ROCKETPREP

I0006810

# AWS Concepts
## 500 Practice Questions

Dominate Your Certification Exams and Interviews

*Zack Austin*

Azure Publishing

**Copyright 2017 by Azure Publishing. All rights reserved.**

ISBN 978-1-387-22078-6

All rights reserved. This work may not be translated or copied in whole or in part without the written permission of the authors. No part of this publication may be reproduced, stored in a retrieval system, or transmitted in any form or by any means-electronic, mechanical, photocopying, scanning, or otherwise-without prior written permission of the authors, except as permitted under Section 107 or 108 of the 1976 United States Copyright Act.

Limit of Liability/Disclaimer of Warranty: While the authors have used their best efforts in preparing this book, they make no representation or warranties with respect to the accuracy or completeness of the contents of this book and specifically disclaim any implied warranties of merchantability or fitness for a particular purpose. No warranty may be created or extended by sales representatives or written sales materials. The advice and strategies contained herein may not be suitable for your situation. You should consult with a professional where appropriate. The authors shall not be liable for any loss of profit or any other commercial damages, including but not limited to special, incidental, consequential, or other damages.

The use in this publication of tradenames, trademarks, service marks, and similar terms, even if they are not identified as such, is not to be taken as an expression of opinion as to whether or not they are subject to proprietary rights.

The following are trademarks of Amazon.com Inc. or its affiliates in the United States and/or other countries: Amazon Web Services, AWS, Amazon Elastic Compute Cloud, Amazon EC2, EC2, Amazon Virtual Private Cloud, Amazon VPC, Amazon S3, Amazon Simple Storage Service, Amazon Cloud-Front, CloudFront, Amazon Simple Queue Service, Amazon SQS, SQS, Amazon Elastic Beanstalk, Amazon Simple Notification Service, Amazon SNS, Amazon Route 53, Amazon Relational Database, Amazon RDS, Amazon Cloud-Watch, AWS Premium Support, Elasticache, Amazon Glacier, AWS Marketplace, AWS CloudFormation, Amazon CloudSearch, Amazon DynamoDB, DynamoDB, Amazon RedShift, and Amazon Kinesis.

Content in this book is not affiliated with or endorsed by Amazon.com Inc. or its affiliates in the United States and/or other countries. Azure Publishing is not associated with any product or vendor mentioned in this book.

CONTENT EDITORS: BHAVANI BHARADWAJ, BAISHALI MANDAL

# Contents

## About The Author

Zack Austin has been building large scale enterprise systems for clients in media, telecom, financial services and publishing since 2001. His current focus is using machine learning to analyze customer behavior in online and offline retail. He is based in New York City.

# Outline

Chapter 1 is about introduction to the AWS cloud computing platform.

Chapter 2 tests you on the content storage services by AWS such as Amazon Simple Storage Service and Amazon Glacier.

Chapter 3 exclusively covers compute and block-level storage services like Amazon Elastic Compute Cloud and Amazon Elastic Block Store.

Chapter 4 deals with AWS Virtual Private Cloud, the custom-defined AWS virtual network service.

Chapter 5 checks your understanding about how Elastic Load Balancing, Amazon Autoscaling, and Amazon CloudWatch services can be used and optimized.

Chapter 6 tests your expertise in securing resources on your AWS account using AWS Identity and Access Management.

Chapter 7 presents questions related to various database services offered by AWS including Amazon RDS and Amazon DynamoDB.

Chapter 8 focuses on application services like Amazon Simple Queue Service, Amazon Simple Notification Service, etc.

Chapter 9 covers Domain Name System (DNS) and Amazon Route 53.

Chapter 10 deals with the in-memory caching service by AWS, Amazon ElastiCache.

Chapter 11 tests your knowledge on other key AWS services like Amazon CloudFront, AWS OpsWorks, Amazon Kinesis, Amazon Elastic Map Reduce

(EMR), and more.

Chapter 12 is about security related concepts that an AWS Solutions Architect is expected to know.

Chapter 13 covers questions on risk and compliance in AWS, shared responsibility model, and risk mitigation.

Chapter 14 tests your knowledge about design principles recommended by AWS, and best practices in architecting applications and systems for the cloud.

1. Which of the following statements is true?

   A. AWS Regions are physical geographic locations with a cluster of data centers that enable deployment of data in multiple locations around the globe.

   B. AZs are physical geographic locations with a cluster of data centers that enable deployment of data in multiple locations around the globe.

   C. AWS Regions are neo-physical locations with a block of data centers that enable computing of data in multiple locations around the globe.

   D. AWS Regions are logical memory locations with a cluster of data sets that enable deployment of data in multiple locations around the globe.

2. Which of the following statements is true?

   A. Ways in which AWS educates customers about AWS security and control environment: By supplying certificates, reports, etc. directly to account owners.

   B. Ways in which AWS educates customers about AWS security and control environment: By storing certificates, reports, etc. and providing them directly to account owners.

   C. Ways in which AWS educates customers about AWS security and control environment: By supplying certificates, reports, etc. directly to customers.

   D. Ways in which AWS educates IAM users about AWS security and control environment: By supplying certificates, reports, etc. directly to customers.

3. Which of the following statements is true?

   A. Amazon Glacier Common Use Cases include: * Backup and archive * Big data analytics * Disaster Recovery

   B. Amazon S3 Common Use Cases include: * Backup and

archive * Big data analytics * Disaster Recovery

C. Amazon S3 Common Use Cases include: * Backup and Restore * Big data analytics * Business Continuity Planning

D. Amazon S3 Common Use Cases include: * Maintenance and Backup * Business analytics * Disaster Recovery

4. Which of the following is an advantage of Cloud Computing?

A. Latent in minutes

B. Scalable in minutes

C. Available in minutes

D. Global in minutes

5. Jack wants to use a Management Tool offered by AWS, what tool should Jack use?

A. Amazon RDS

B. AWS CloudTrail

C. Amazon VPC

D. Amazon ElastiCache

6. What is the characteristic of an Internal load balancer in ELB?

A. Internal load balancer balances load between the tiers of a multi-tier application. E.g. Routes traffic to EC2 instances in VPCs with private subnets.

B. Internal load balancer encrypts data between clients who initiate HTTPS sessions and a load balancer.

C. Internal load balancer encrypts data between clients who initiate SSH sessions and a load balancer.

D. Internal load balancer in ELB takes requests from clients over the Internet, and allocates them to EC2 instances registered with the load balancer.

7. Which of the following statements is true?

A. List of AWS Architecture Best Practices: * Designing for security processes. * Decoupling elasticity.

B. List of AWS Architecture Best Practices: * Designing for parallelization * Decoupling application components.

C. List of AWS Architecture Best Practices: * Designing for failure. * Decoupling application components.

D. List of AWS Architecture Best Practices: * Designing for integrity. * Decoupling security components.

8. Which of the following statements is true?

A. IAM is an operating system identity management where the users can access an AWS account through the operating system console.

B. IAM enables granular level control over the data and applications in an AWS account as defined by the root user.

C. IAM enables granular level control over the people and applications that can access an AWS account.

D. IAM enables operational level control over the people and applications that can access an AWS account through the CLI.

9. How can building a highly available architecture on AWS be achieved?

   A. A Highly available architecture on AWS can be achieved by building systems that can withstand the failure of single or multiple components.

   B. A Highly available architecture on AWS can be achieved by building processes that ensure confidentiality and integrity of resources.

   C. A Highly available architecture on AWS can be achieved by building systems that do not violate the AWS Acceptable Use policy.

   D. A Highly available architecture on AWS can be achieved by building systems that are operationally effective of IT controls.

10. Which of the following is a primary cloud computing deployment model?

   A. Neutron Hybrid Deployment

   B. Composite Deployment

   C. Hybrid Deployment

   D. Sandbox Deployment

11. Which of the following statements is true?

   A. List of Database Services offered by AWS: Amazon RDS MongoDB Amazon Redshift

   B. List of Compute and Networking services offered by AWS: Amazon RDS Amazon DynamoDB Amazon Redshift

   C. List of Database Services offered by AWS: Amazon RDS Amazon DynamoDB Amazon Redshift

   D. List of Database Services offered by AWS: Amazon VPC Amazon DynamoDB Amazon Redshift

12. What is the characteristic of an Internet-facing load balancer in ELB?

   A. Internet-facing load balancer encrypts data between clients who initiate SSH sessions and a load balancer.

   B. Internet-facing load balancer balances load between the tiers of a multi-tier application. E.g. Routes traffic to EC2 instances in VPCs with private subnets.

   C. Internet-facing load balancer encrypts data between clients who initiate HTTPS sessions and a load balancer.

   D. Internet-facing load balancer in ELB takes requests from clients over the Internet, and allocates them to EC2 instances registered with the load balancer.

13. Which of the following statements is true?

   A. List of Compute and Networking services offered by AWS: Amazon S3 Amazon Glacier Amazon EBS

   B. List of Storage and Content Delivery services offered by AWS: Amazon S3 Amazon Glacier Amazon EBS

   C. List of Storage and Content Delivery services offered by AWS: Amazon S3 Amazon Glacier Amazon VPC

   D. List of Storage and Content Delivery services offered by AWS: AWS Lambda Amazon Glacier Amazon EBS

14. What is a Maintenance Window?

    A. Maintenance Window is the 60 minute time duration specified during configuration when either requested or required software updates occur in Amazon ElastiCache.

    B. Maintenance Window is the 120 minute time duration specified by the customer when either requested or required software patching occurs in Amazon ElastiCache.

    C. Maintenance Window is the 60 minute time duration specified by the customer when either requested or required software patching occurs in Amazon ElastiCache.

    D. Maintenance Window is the 60 minute time duration specified by the account owner when either requested or required data backups are taken in Amazon ElastiCache.

15. Which of the following statements is true?

    A. Security Standards and Certifications AWS is in compliance with: * PSA * DIACAP * ISO 9001, ISO 22000, and ISO 27001

    B. Security Standards and Certifications AWS is in compliance with: * IANA * DIACAP * ISO 9002, ISO 27001, and ISO 27018

    C. Security Standards and Certifications AWS is in compliance with: * FISMA * GSA * ISO 9002, ISO 22000, and ISO 27018

    D. Security Standards and Certifications AWS is in compliance with: * FISMA * DIACAP * ISO 9001, ISO 27001, and ISO 27018

16. Which of the following statements is true?

    A. Benefits of AZs: Low-latency, cost-effective connectivity to other AZs within a region.

    B. Benefits of AZs: Low-latency, cost-effective computing to other AZs within a region.

    C. Benefits of AZs: Low-scalability, cost-effective connectivity to other AZs within a region.

    D. Benefits of AWS Regions: Low-latency, cost-effective connectivity to other AZs within a region.

17. Which of the following statements is true?

    A. Hybrid model is a service that connects infrastructure and functions between new resources located in the cloud and the cloud-based resources.

    B. Hybrid model is an architectural pattern that connects infrastructure and applications between existing resources not located in the cloud and the cloud-based resources.

    C. All-in Deployment model is an architectural pattern that connects infrastructure and applications between existing resources not located in the cloud and the cloud-based resources.

D. Hybrid model is a composite pattern that merges infrastructure and applications between existing regions not located in the cloud and the cloud-based resources.

18. Which of the following describes a way in which AWS educates customers about AWS security and control environment?

    A. By offering functionalities, services etc. directly to customers.

    B. By acquiring industry standard certifications and 3rd party attestations.

    C. By supplying certificates, reports, etc. directly to account owners.

    D. By acquiring industry standard certifications and account owner attestation.

19. Which of the following is a Security and Identity service offered by AWS?

    A. AWS IAM

    B. AWS CloudTrail

    C. AWS Lambda

    D. AWS Config

20. Which of the following statements is true?

    A. You can integrate CloudHSM with Amazon RDS only for DB2 instances, allowing AWS to operate DB2 databases while you still control master encryption keys.

    B. You can integrate CloudHSM with Amazon RDS only for Oracle instances, allowing AWS to operate Oracle databases while you

still control master encryption keys.

    C. You can integrate CloudHSM with Redshift only for Oracle instances, allowing AWS to operate Oracle databases while you still control master encryption keys.

    D. You can integrate CloudHSM with Amazon VPC only for EC2 instances, allowing AWS to operate EC2 databases while you still control master encryption keys.

21. Meg wants to access AWS cloud services platform, How should Meg access the services?

    A. You can access AWS cloud services platform using one of these: AWS console UI AWS REST API AWS Software Development Kits (SDKs)

    B. You can access AWS cloud services platform using one of these: AWS management console AWS Dual-Stack Interface (DLI) AWS Simple Development Kits (SDKs)

    C. You can access AWS cloud services platform using one of these: AWS management console AWS Command Line Interface (CLI) AWS Software Development Kits (SDKs)

    D. You can access AWS cloud services platform using one of these: AWS management console AWS Command Line Interface (CLI) AWS Control Lists (ACLs)

22. Which of the following statements is true?

A. List of Management Tools offered by AWS: Amazon API Gateway Amazon Elastic Transcoder Amazon SNS

B. List of Application Services offered by AWS: Amazon API Gateway Amazon ElastiCache Amazon SNS

C. List of Security and Identity offered by AWS: Amazon API Gateway Amazon Elastic Transcoder Amazon SNS

D. List of Application Services offered by AWS: Amazon API Gateway Amazon Elastic Transcoder Amazon SNS

23. What is All-in Deployment Model?

A. All-in Deployment Model is an architectural pattern that connects all its components and resources, which is located in the cloud.

B. All-in Deployment Model is an architectural pattern that connects applications between existing resources not located in the cloud and the cloud-based resources.

C. All-in Deployment Model is an application that is completely deployed in the cloud, with all its components running in the cloud.

D. All-in Deployment Model is an application that is completely deployed in the cloud, with its components connect to an architectural pattern.

24. What is Amazon S3?

A. Amazon S3 is a low-cost cloud storage service that offers long-term backup and supports lifecycle policies supporting automatic migration among storage classes.

B. Amazon S3 is a web service that helps to coordinate messages and enables applications to send and receive notifications from the cloud.

C. Amazon S3 is the core object storage service on AWS that offers unlimited data storage and high durability.

D. Amazon S3 is a web service solution that helps host multi-platform applications.

25. Which of the following is an advantage of Cloud Computing?

A. Economies of scale

B. Highly Latent

C. Fixed vs. capital expense

D. Focuses on functional differentiators

# Content Storage

*2*

1. Which of the following statements is true?

   A. Performing a GET on an object with a delete marker returns a 404 error and an 'x-amz-delete-marker: true' header.

   B. Performing a PUT/LIST on an object with a delete marker returns a 404 error and an 'x-amz-delete-marker: true' header.

   C. Performing a GET on an object with a delete marker returns a 404 error and an 'x-amz-delete-marker: false' header.

   D. Performing a GET on an object with a delete marker returns a 503 error and an 'x-amz-delete-marker: true' header.

2. Which of the following describes the permission contexts which are evaluated for account owners and IAM users when they perform an operation on an S3 object?

   A. Permission contexts evaluated for both account owners and IAM users when they perform an operation on an S3 object: User context Object context

   B. Permission contexts evaluated for both account owners and IAM users when they perform an operation on an S3 object: User context Bucket context Object context

   C. Permission contexts evaluated for both account owners and IAM users when they perform an operation on an S3 object: User context Bucket context

   D. Permission contexts evaluated for both account owners and IAM users when they perform an operation on an S3 object: Group context Bucket context Object context

3. What is the Maximum expiration for a pre-signed S3 URL?

   A. 24 hours

B. 48 hours

C. Multiple years

D. 1 year

4. Ida wants to know how to encrypt Amazon S3 data, how should Ida attempt S3 Encryption?

   A. Either server-side or client-side encryptions can be used for data stored on S3, and document the encryption process with Amazon LMS.

   B. Either server-side or client-side encryptions can be used for data stored on S3, with Amazon KMS managing the encryption keys.

   C. Use server-side encryption or protect data in transit stored on S3 by using TLS.

   D. Use server-side encryption or protect data in transit stored on S3 by implementing reactive security controls.

5. Which of the following describes the permission context which is evaluated when an account owner performs an operation on an S3 bucket owned by the owner?

   A. Group context

   B. Bucket context

   C. User context

   D. Object context

6. Which of the following statements is true?

   A. A bucket policy can control access to specific S3 objects.

   B. A bucket policy can access S3 objects only if they are the object owners.

   C. A bucket policy cannot control access to specific S3 objects.

   D. A bucket policy can control access to all S3 objects.

7. Which of the following statements is true?

   A. Amazon Glacier Common Use Cases include: * Backup and archive * Big data analytics * Disaster Recovery

   B. Amazon S3 Common Use Cases include: * Backup and archive * Big data analytics * Disaster Recovery

   C. Amazon S3 Common Use Cases include: * Backup and Restore * Big data analytics * Business Continuity Planning

   D. Amazon S3 Common Use Cases include: * Maintenance and Backup * Business analytics * Disaster Recovery

8. What are the characteristics of Amazon Server Access Logs?

   A. Amazon Server Access logs are enabled to track requests sent to an S3 bucket and provide details like the requestor, time, object, action, response, etc.

   B. Amazon Server Access logs are enabled to track requests sent to an S3 bucket, and the logs can be stored in the same bucket only.

   C. Amazon Server Access logs are enabled to track requests sent to an S3 bucket and provide details like the account owner, pre-signed URL details, and error codes.

D. Amazon Server Access logs are enabled to track requests sent to an S3 bucket and and provides details of the usage and performance of objects.

9. Mia wants to know how to delete objects permanently when the versioning is on, how should Mia attempt this?

A. Permanent deletion of an object is possible even when versioning is enabled if the object is flagged for deletion with the delete marker.

B. Permanent deletion of an object is possible even when versioning is enabled if the S3.EXPIRE.OBJECT record is generated.

C. Permanent deletion of an object is possible even when versioning is enabled if the object is marked as non-current.

D. Permanent deletion of an object is possible even when versioning is enabled if the version ID is included in the DELETE request.

10. Which of the following is a best practice to maximize the performance of S3?

A. Use AWS Lambda

B. Use CloudFront

C. Use MFA generated authentication codes to distribute data

D. Store objects by using the string values of the object key names which are stored alphabetically as an index.

11. Which of the following is a step to enable Static Web Hosting on S3?

A. Autoscale and Load Balance the website.

B. Provide persistent file system for virtual server.

C. Create new stack.

D. Create a bucket with the website hostname.

12. Which of the following statements is true?

A. AWS regions for the S3 buckets can be assigned by the object owners and data will be stored in that region unless a customer explicitly moves it to a different region.

B. AWS regions for the S3 buckets can be randomly chosen by the customers and data will be moved in that region unless an account owner explicitly transfers it to a different region.

C. AWS regions for the S3 objects can be chosen by the customers and data will be stored in that region unless a customer explicitly copies it to a different region.

D. AWS regions for the S3 buckets can be chosen by the customers and data will be stored in that region unless a customer explicitly copies it to a different region.

13. Which of the following describes a valid option to implement S3 encryption?

A. Client-side encryption with KMS-managed keys .

B. Client-side encryption using TLS.

C. Client-side encryption with S3-managed keys.

D. Client-side encryption using FTPS.

14. What is the use of prefix and delimiter parameters?

    A. Prefixes and Delimiters are used as a convention to identify key names.
    B. Prefixes and Delimiters are used in listing key names.
    C. Prefixes and Delimiters are used to denote full paths of directories.
    D. Prefixes and Delimiters are used in sorting folders and subfolders.

15. Which of the following describes a countermeasure for the poor performance caused by S3 access patterns?

    A. Using sequenced key name prefixes and key names.
    B. Using CloudFront to reduce load.
    C. Using sequenced prefixes in key names.
    D. Using alphabetically sequenced key names.

16. Noe was searching for the creation of one-time pre-signed S3 download links, what should Noe know about the creation of the download links?

    A. It is not possible to create a one-time pre-signed S3 download link, but a pre-signed URL with an expiration assigned by account owner can be created.
    B. Account owners can create a one-time pre-signed S3 download link, and a pre-signed URL with a very short expiration.

    C. It is not possible to create a one-time pre-signed S3 download link, but a pre-signed URL with a long-term expiration can be created.
    D. It is not possible to create a one-time pre-signed S3 download link, but a pre-signed URL with a very short expiration can be created.

17. Amy is facing a partial upload failure of a single part of a multipart S3, how can Amy resolve this situation?

    A. If a single part of a multipart S3 upload fails, the entire process needs to be restarted.
    B. If a single part of a multipart S3 upload fails, it is possible to retry the upload of that part by specifying the part number.
    C. If a single part of a multipart S3 upload fails, the upload will be aborted.
    D. If a single part of a multipart S3 upload fails, the account owner to retry the upload of that part by specifying the part number from 1 to 100,000.

18. What is Object Storage?

    A. Object Storage is a type of data storage in which the data is managed at device level as addressable blocks.
    B. Object Storage is a type of data storage in which the data is managed as objects that comprise both data and metadata, manipulated by an API.

C. Object storage is a type of data storage in which the data is recorded on a readable medium using infrastructure provisioning.

D. Object Storage is a type of data storage in which the data is managed at the OS level as files and folders.

19. Which of the following describes a Bucket owner's rights on objects not owned by them?

A. If an object in a bucket is not owned by the bucket owner, the owner: Can delegate it.

B. If an object in a bucket is not owned by the bucket owner, the owner: Can deactivate it.

C. If an object in a bucket is not owned by the bucket owner, the owner: Cannot write to it.

D. If an object in a bucket is not owned by the bucket owner, the owner: Can deny access to it

20. What is a Cross-region replication?

A. Cross-region replication is a feature that allows asynchronous replication of new objects from a source bucket in an AWS region to a target bucket in a different region.

B. Cross-region replication is a feature that allows the creation of multiple VPCs within the same region or in different regions and ensures high availability.

C. Cross-region replication is a feature that offers virtual networking capabilities where users can provision isolated networks to host AWS resources.

D. Cross-region replication allows synchronous replication of existing objects from a source bucket in an AWS region to any other target bucket.

21. Which of the following statements is true?

A. Mechanisms to secure S3 data are: * Strong bucket policies * Using secure stored versions * Consolidating identities from internal IdPs

B. Mechanisms to secure S3 data are: * Strong bucket policies * MFA delete and versioning * Creating a separate account to store objects and using cross-account access

C. Mechanisms to secure S3 data are: * Strong IAM policies * Deleting old keys * Creating a separate account to store objects and using cross-account access

D. Mechanisms to authenticate S3 accounts are: * Strong bucket policies * MFA delete and versioning * Creating a separate account to store objects and using cross-account access

22. Which of the following is a step to retrieve an archive for Glacier?

A. Use API calls by passing the object id.

B. Send a request to the account owner to download the bytes.

C. Protect overwriting by using WORM.

D. Initiate an archive retrieval job.

23. Which of the following describes the permission context that is evaluated when an IAM user performs an operation on an S3 bucket, owned by its parent account?

    A. Permission contexts evaluated when an IAM user performs an operation on an S3 bucket that is owned by its parent account: User context Bucket context

    B. Permission context evaluated when an IAM user performs an operation on an S3 bucket that is owned by its parent account: Bucket context

    C. Permission contexts evaluated when an IAM user performs an operation on an S3 bucket that is owned by its parent account: User context Object context

    D. Permission context evaluated when an IAM user performs an operation on an S3 bucket that is owned by its parent account: User context

24. Which of the following best describes who can be granted controlled access to Amazon S3 objects?

    A. Controlled access may be granted to anyone using canned ACLs.

    B. Controlled access may be granted to anyone having temporary security credentials.

    C. Controlled access may be granted to anyone using S3 bucket policies, ACLs, and AWS IAM.

    D. Controlled access may be granted to anyone using ACPs.

25. Which of the following best describes a use case of an Amazon S3 storage class?

    A. Standard-IA: For archives and long-term backups.

    B. Amazon S3 Standard: For easily reproduced data.

    C. RRS storage class: For general purpose data that requires high performance and low latency.

    D. Amazon S3 Standard: For general purpose data that requires high performance and low latency.

26. Ben is an account owner who wants to grant Tom, another account owner access to an S3 resource, can Tom grant access of the same resource to some other owner?

    A. Recipient of delegated permission can only further delegate permission to users in their account and not to the owner of a different AWS account.

    B. Recipient of delegated permission can further delegate permission both to users in their account and to the owner of a different AWS account.

    C. Recipient of delegated permission cannot further delegate permission to users in their account but only to the owner of a different AWS account.

D. Recipient of delegated permission cannot further delegate permission to users in their account or the owner of a different AWS account.

27. What is a Multipart Upload API?

A. Multipart Upload API is the API that allows multiple objects to be merged as a single set and uploaded as a contiguous portion of an object.

B. Multipart Upload API is the API that allows uploading of an object and has a very short expiry period, with the upload being aborted only by an account owner.

C. Multipart Upload API is the API that allows for large objects to be copied/uploaded as a set of parts, providing better network utilization, and the ability to pause and resume.

D. Multipart Upload API is the API that allows BLOBs to be created and uploaded in parts, providing an optimized way to independently upload the object.

28. Which of the following statements is true?

A. S3 supports bucket policies, where flagged objects in a bucket can override the use server-side encryption.

B. S3 supports IAM policies, where flagged objects in a bucket can be mandated to use server-side encryption.

C. S3 supports object policies where all objects in a bucket can be mandated to use client-side encryption.

D. S3 supports bucket policies where all objects in a bucket can be mandated to use server-side encryption.

29. What are the characteristics of Vaults in Amazon Glacier?

A. Vaults are inventories of archives and an AWS account can have upto 10,000 vaults with each vault storing unlimited number of archives.

B. Vaults are placeholders for archives and an AWS account can have upto 2,000 vaults with each vault storing archives up to 100TB of data.

C. Vaults are containers for archives and an AWS account can have upto 1,000 vaults with each vault storing unlimited number of archives.

D. Vaults are storage classes for archives and an AWS account can have upto 3,000 vaults with each vault having the capacity to store up to 40TB of data.

30. What can you expect when an S3 object's expiration policy is triggered and the versioning is not on?

A. When the versioning is not on, the object is deleted.

B. When the versioning is not on, the object is flagged for deletion.

C. When the versioning is not on, the object is not deleted.

D. When the versioning is not on, the S3.EXPIRE.OBJECT record is generated.

31. How is the storage partition of objects determined in S3?

   A. The storage partition of objects in S3 is determined by a clustered index referenced by a DDL.

   B. The storage partition of objects in S3 is determined by a process of mounting a partition and accessing the functional volumes.

   C. The storage partition of objects in S3 is determined by an index-organized table subdivided into smaller pieces called partitions which reside in tablespaces.

   D. The storage partition of objects in S3 is determined by the string values of the object key names which are stored alphabetically as an index.

32. What are the characteristics of Pre-signed URLs?

   A. Pre-Signed URLs protect media and other web content against unauthorized web scraping by granting time-limited permissions to download objects.

   B. Pre-Signed URLs protect web content scrapping by sharing long-term security credentials with account owners and federated users.

   C. Pre-Signed URLs protect users and other account owners against unauthorized web access by granting time-limited permissions to download objects.

   D. Pre-Signed URLs allow object owners to share objects after generating authentication code by MFA device and sharing the code to download objects.

33. What is the data consistency model that is employed by Amazon S3?

   A. Amazon S3 offers eventual data consistency for overwrite PUTs and Deletes, and for PUTs of new objects it provides read-after-write consistency.

   B. Amazon S3 offers perpetual data consistency for PUTs and Deletes of new objects, and for GETs of new objects it provides read-after-write consistency.

   C. Amazon S3 offers eventual data consistency for overwrite LISTs and GETs, and for PUTs and GETs of new object it provides read-after-write consistency.

   D. Amazon S3 offers eventual data consistency for overwrite GETs, and for PUTs and LISTs of new object it provides read-after-write consistency.

34. What are the characteristics of Range GETs?

   A. Range GETs allows users to cache a set of objects in a given range of bytes to cater to download requests.

   B. Range GETs allows users to download (GET) only the required portion of an object instead of having to download the entire object.

   C. Range GETs allows users to download (GET) only from the cache, if it contains any objects then downloads are catered, otherwise, it results in failed transfers.

D. Range GETs allows users to download (GET) from archives a portion of data that the user specifies through part numbers.

35. Rex is exploring spike in S3 request rates, what should Rex do when there is a very large and sudden spike in request rates?

A. When very large spikes in S3 requests rates are expected, use a CDN for the extra load.

B. When very large spikes in S3 requests rates are expected, a support case can be submitted to Amazon so they can prepare for the extra load.

C. When very large spikes in S3 requests are expected, use reserved instances to handle the temporary overload.

D. When very large spikes in S3 requests rates are expected, process requests asynchronously with some delay.

36. What is the encryption level of S3 objects?

A. All S3 objects are encrypted at the server-side, at the object level, and not the block level.

B. All S3 objects are encrypted with a secret key, at the bucket level, and not the object level.

C. All S3 objects are encrypted with a unique key at the object level, and not the bucket level.

D. All S3 objects are encrypted at the client-side, at the bucket level, and not the block level.

37. Which of the following statements is true?

A. Replicated: Objects encrypted (server-side) using SSE-S3 and AES-128 block cipher, and their versions.

B. Replicated: Objects encrypted (client-side) using SSL.

C. Replicated: Objects encrypted (server-side) using Amazon S3 managed encryption keys, and their versions.

D. Replicated: Objects encrypted (client-side) using AES-256 block cipher.

38. What should the byte range be for range retrievals in Glacier?

A. The byte range should begin at 1 byte or any 10MB interval thereafter, and end at the end of the archive or any 10MB interval greater than the beginning range.

B. The byte range should begin at 1 byte or any 1GB interval thereafter, and end at the end of the archive or any 10GB interval greater than the beginning range.

C. The byte range should begin at 0 or any 1TB interval thereafter, and end at the end of the archive or any 1TB interval greater than the beginning range.

D. The byte range should begin at 0 or any 1MB interval thereafter, and end at the end of the archive or any 1MB interval greater than the beginning range.

39. How is a Key defined?

A. Key is a unique identifier that identifies every S3 object in a bucket, and can be upto 1034 bytes of Unicode UTF-16 and 32 encodings.

B. Key is a unique identifier that identifies every S3 object in a bucket, and can be upto 255 bytes of Unicode UTF-16 encodings.

C. Key is a unique identifier that identifies every S3 object in a bucket, and can be upto 1024 bytes of Unicode UTF-8 characters like embedded slashes, backslashes, etc.

D. Key is a unique identifier that identifies every S3 object in a bucket, and can be upto 1700 bytes of Unicode UTF-32 encodings.

40. Which of the following statements is true?

A. Best practices to maximize S3 performance: * Use CloudFront * Store objects by using the string values of the object key names which are stored alphabetically as an index

B. Best practices to maximize S3 performance: * Use CloudFront * Use multipart PUTs to maximize bandwidth

C. Best practices to maximize DynamoDB performance: * Use CloudFront * Use multipart PUTs to maximize bandwidth

D. Best practices to maximize S3 performance: * Use AWS Lambda * Use multipart PUTs to maximize bandwidth

41. What are the characteristics of Amazon S3 Versioning?

A. S3 versioning technology allows the existence of several versions and also supports retention of old copies of data.

B. S3 versioning technology assigns objects with unique version names which are sequence-based and used to collaborate data easily.

C. S3 technology keeps multiple versions with assigned numbers in categories marked as Major, Minor, Patch to fix bugs and also provide backward-compatibility.

D. S3 technology keeps multiple retrievable versions of all objects (marked with unique version IDs) to protect data against malicious or accidental deletion.

42. Gia is searching for multifactor authentication used by S3 server-side encryption, what safeguards are used to protect the data at rest?

A. S3 server-side encryption uses stream cipher that encrypts objects with the secret key and generated authentication key codes.

B. S3 server-side encryption uses symmetric key cipher that encrypts each object with a unique key, and each key with a master key that is regularly rotated.

C. S3 server-side encryption uses AES-256 block cipher that encrypts each object with a unique key, and each key with a master key that is regularly rotated.

D. S3 server-side encryption uses AES-128 block cipher that encrypts objects with the secret key, and generates enforcement key codes.

43. Eva is searching for encryption of object metadata, what should Eva know about S3 server-side encryption on object metadata?

A. S3 only provides server-side encryption of the objects in the bucket, not the metadata.

B. S3 only provides server-side encryption of the objects in the bucket and the metadata using TLS.

C. S3 only provides server-side encryption of the objects in the bucket by implementing reactive security controls, not the metadata.

D. S3 only provides server-side encryption of both the objects in the bucket and the metadata.

44. What is Block Storage?

A. Block storage is a type of data storage in which the data is recorded on a readable medium using infrastructure provisioning.

B. Block Storage is a type of data storage in which the data is managed at device level as addressable blocks.

C. Block Storage is a type of data storage in which the data is managed at the OS level as files and folders.

D. Block Storage is a type of data storage in which the data is managed as objects that comprise both data and metadata, manipulated by an API.

45. What operations are protected by MFA Delete?

A. Changing the references to an object marked for deletion.

B. Permanent deletion of an object version.

C. Changing an object's state to null when marked for deletion.

D. Permanent deletion of a non-versioned object.

46. What is not replicated by Amazon S3?

A. Not replicated: Objects tags.

B. Not replicated: Objects in a source bucket with or without bucket owner having permissions.

C. Not replicated: Objects encrypted (server-side) using Amazon S3 managed encryption keys, and their versions.

D. Not replicated: Objects encrypted (server-side) using customer provided or AWS KMS managed encryption keys.

47. What is the key characteristic of Amazon Glacier?

A. Supports objects upto 5TB.

B. Encryption at rest is optional.

C. Objects are identified by customizable key names.

D. Archives are identified by system-generated archive IDs.

48. Which of the following statements is true?

    A. With delegated permission, only an account user can modify a policy on a bucket in another AWS account.

    B. With delegated permission, a user can modify a policy on a bucket in another AWS account.

    C. With delegated permission, only group users can modify a policy on a bucket in another AWS account.

    D. With delegated permission, a federated user can modify a policy on a bucket in another AWS account.

49. What can you expect if the Versioning is set on or is suspended?

    A. Versioning on/suspended: Current version of the object generates S3.EXPIRE.OBJECT record and all non-current versions are archived.

    B. Versioning on/suspended: Current version of the object is made non-current and permanently deleted; and all non-current versions are saved.

    C. Versioning on/suspended: Current version of the object is made non-current by adding a delete marker; and all non-current versions are saved.

    D. Versioning on/suspended: Current version of the object is flagged with a delete marker; and all existing versions are saved.

50. Which of the following describes a countermeasure for the poor performance caused by S3 access patterns?

    A. Using alphabetically sequenced key names.

    B. Reversing key names.

    C. Using sequenced prefixes in key names.

    D. Using sequenced key name prefixes and key names.

51. Ron wants to know how the S3 bucket policies are applied to API calls, what are the credentials used for the S3 bucket policies?

    A. In Amazon S3, bucket policies applied to API calls are written with the credentials of the user authenticated by MFA device.

    B. In Amazon S3, bucket policies applied to API calls are written with the credentials of the authenticated user.

    C. In Amazon S3, bucket policies applied to API calls are written with the credentials of the user authenticated by account owner.

    D. In Amazon S3, bucket policies applied to API calls are written with the credentials of the account owner.

52. Which of the following statements is true?

A. It is possible to use cross-region replication in S3 to replicate objects from a bucket in one AWS account to a bucket in another AWS account via account owner's credentials.

B. It is possible to use cross-region replication in S3 to replicate objects from a bucket in one AWS account to a bucket in another AWS account.

C. It is not possible to use cross-region replication in S3 to replicate objects from a bucket in one AWS account to a bucket in another AWS account.

D. It is possible to use cross-region replication in S3 to replicate objects from a bucket in one AWS account with or without bucket owner's permissions to a bucket in another AWS account.

53. What is the characteristic of the Object Lifecycle Management?

A. Object Lifecycle Management enables hierarchical organization of objects and navigation of data based on time.

B. Object Lifecycle Management enables archiving data and providing backups for objects created.

C. Object Lifecycle Management enables users to access the local object store by authenticating against the AWS Management Console.

D. Object Lifecycle Management enables automatic transitioning of data between storage classes and even data deletion based on time.

54. Which of the following statements is true?

A. Amazon Standard-IA: For archives and long-term backups that are seldom accessed (offers high durability and a retrieval time of 3 to 5 hours)

B. Amazon Glacier: For archives and less frequently accessed data (offers high availability and a retrieval time of 2 to 5 hours)

C. RRS storage class: For archives and long-term backups that are seldom accessed (offers high durability and a retrieval time of 3 to 5 hours)

D. Amazon Glacier: For archives and long-term backups that are seldom accessed (offers high durability and a retrieval time of 3 to 5 hours)

55. Which of the following statements is true?

A. The largest archive that can be uploaded onto a Glacier archive in a multi-part upload request cannot be more than 40GB in size.

B. The largest archive that can be uploaded onto an S3 archive in a single upload request cannot be more than 4GB in size.

C. The largest archive that can be uploaded onto a Glacier archive in a single upload request cannot be more than 4GB in size.

D. The largest archive that can be stored onto a Glacier archive cannot be more than 4TB in size.

56. How much time does it take for a retrieval job to be completed on Glacier?

    A. It takes 4 to 6 hours to for a retrieval job to be completed on Glacier.

    B. It takes 2 to 3 hours to for a retrieval job to be completed on Glacier.

    C. It takes 2 to 4 hours to for a retrieval job to be completed on Glacier.

    D. It takes 3 to 5 hours to for a retrieval job to be completed on Glacier.

57. What is the maximum size for S3 objects that can be downloaded through BitTorrent?

    A. The maximum size of Bit-Torrent downloadable objects is 5 GB.

    B. The maximum size of Bit-Torrent downloadable objects is 5 TB.

    C. The maximum size of Bit-Torrent downloadable objects is 10 GB.

    D. The maximum size of Bit-Torrent downloadable objects is 10 MB.

58. What is Amazon Glacier?

    A. Amazon Glacier is a web service solution that helps host multi-platform applications.

    B. Amazon Glacier is the core object storage service on AWS that offers unlimited data storage and high durability.

    C. Amazon Glacier is a web service that helps to coordinate messages and enables applications to send and receive notifications from the cloud.

    D. Amazon Glacier is a low-cost storage service with secure, durable, and flexible storage solutions for online backup and data archiving.

59. Which of the following statements is true?

    A. Amazon Glacier does not multipart upload.

    B. Amazon 3 supports multipart uploads, and it is recommended for archives over 100MB in size.

    C. Amazon Glacier supports multipart uploads, and it is recommended for archives over 250MB in size.

    D. Amazon Glacier supports multipart uploads, and it is recommended for archives over 100MB in size.

60. Which of the following describes the ordering of the response from S3 GET Bucket operation?

    A. The operation in S3 which returns a list of randomized key name prefixes.

    B. The operation in S3 which returns a list of randomized key names.

    C. The operation in S3 which returns a list of randomized key name prefixes and key names.

    D. The operation in S3 which returns a list of key names sequenced alphabetically.

61. What are the characteristics of Amazon S3 Event notifications?

A. Event notifications are set up at bucket level to send responses supported by Amazon SQS/SNS and AWS Lambda, to track and analyze the performance in objects in S3.

B. Event notifications are set up through object lifecycle policies to send responses supported by Amazon SQS/SNS and AWS Lambda, to track the changes in objects in S3.

C. Event notifications are set up at object level to enable receiving notifications of events through the entire object lifecycle and supported by Amazon SNS, AWS Lambda.

D. Event notifications are set up at bucket level to send responses (like Amazon SQS/SNS messages or trigger a Lambda function) to create/delete actions taken on objects stored in S3.

# 3

## Compute and Block Storage

1. What is AMI?

   A. AMI defines the directory structure with files and has instances of the executables and data files related to your applications.

   B. AMI defines the initial software state of an instance at the time of launch including OS and configuration, initial state of patches, and application/system software.

   C. AMI defines the initial software state of an instance during launch, including algorithms to be applied to input data, and permissions to control AWS accounts.

   D. AMI defines the backup process for a virtual machine (VM) and creates copies of the system state and application configurations.

2. Which of the following describes what the R3 Instance Type is best suited for?

   A. Development environments

   B. MPP data warehousing

   C. Distributed memory caches

   D. Data Warehousing

3. Eli is trying to detach an EC2 instance's primary ENI, how should Eli attempt detaching the Primary ENI of an EC2 Instance?

   A. The Primary ENI cannot be detached from an EC2 instance, but you can associate it with a subnet range to a network interface.

   B. The Primary ENI cannot be detached from an EC2 instance, but you can create additional ENIs and attach them to the instance.

   C. The Primary ENI cannot be detached from an EC2 instance, but you can create a management network to manage the instances.

   D. The Primary ENI can be detached from an EC2 instance by creating a network interface.

4. How can you launch an EC2 Instance?

A. You can launch an Amazon EC2 instance by specifying the root device and the reference id of the instance.

B. You can launch an Amazon EC2 instance by specifying the source of the AMI and an instance type.

C. You can launch an Amazon EC2 instance by specifying an AMI and an instance type.

D. You can launch an Amazon EC2 instance by specifying an existing EC2 instance and its type.

5. Which of the following is a characteristic of a Security Group Rule?

A. Applied at the subnet level

B. Rules cannot be aggregated to create one single set

C. Deny by default

D. Stateless

6. What are Instances?

A. Instances are virtual servers through the launching of which Amazon EC2 helps acquire your required compute, Amazon charges you on an hourly basis for the use of instances.

B. Instances are launched using an HVM AMI that helps acquire the required compute, and the instances are available on-demand and charged on a monthly basis.

C. Instances are designed to improve the performance of your workload by providing a moderate baseline performance, and the instances are free within specific usage limits.

D. Instances are designed to store instances of large binary files and cater particularly to content storage.

7. What are the data transfer charges between instances in different AZs?

A. If you are transferring data from an instance in one AZ to an instance in another, charges up to a specified limit will not apply, and later the data in-out charges will apply.

B. If you are transferring data from an instance in one AZ to an instance in another, you will be charged out for the former and in for the latter.

C. If you are transferring data from an instance in one AZ to an instance in another, you will be charged for the transfer as Internet Data Transfer, on both the sides.

D. If you are transferring data from an instance in one AZ to an instance in another, you will be charged in for the first instance and charged out for the second instance.

8. What is the maximum number of accumulated CPU credits for the instance type T2.medium of the T2 (burstable) server class?

A. 24 hours of credits. Which means: T2.micro - 72 (3 CPU Credits/hr * 24) T2.small - 144 (6 CPU Credits / hr * 24) T2.medium - 216 (9 CPU Credits / hr * 24)

B. 24 hours of credits. Which means: T2.micro - 144 (6 CPU Credits/hr * 24) T2.small - 288 (12 CPU Credits / hr * 24) T2.medium - 432 (18 CPU Credits / hr * 24)

C. 24 hours of credits. Which means: T2.micro - 144 (6 CPU Credits/hr * 24) T2.small - 288 (12 CPU Credits / hr * 24) T2.medium - 576 (24 CPU Credits / hr * 24)

D. 24 hours of credits. Which means: T2.micro - 144 (6 CPU Credits/hr * 24) T2.small - 216 (9 CPU Credits / hr * 24) T2.medium - 288 (12 CPU Credits / hr * 24)

9. Which of the following statements is true?

A. EC2 Instance Profile is a container for IAM users which can be used to associate IAM groups to an EC2 instance at instance start-up.

B. EC2 Instance Profile is an identifier for IAM groups which can be used to associate users to an EC2 instance at instance start-up.

C. EC2 Instance Profile is an identifier for IAM roles which can be used to find out unique roles of an EC2 instance at instance start-up.

D. EC2 Instance Profile is a container for IAM roles which can be used to associate roles to an EC2 instance at instance start-up.

10. What is the default maximum number of EC2-Classic security groups per instance?

A. 100

B. 300

C. 500

D. 5

11. Which of the following describes what the T2 (burstable) server class is best suited for?

A. High-traffic web applications

B. Monitor servers

C. Very Large databases

D. Development environments

12. Which of the following describes a modification that can be done on an existing RI?

A. Changing instance type that is either active or not active.

B. Changing instance type within an instance family.

C. Changing the subnet association utilization options.

D. Changing instance type to another instance family, like Windows RI.

13. What are Instance Stores?

A. Instance Stores are persistent block storage located virtually, included with the hourly cost of your instance.

B. Instance Stores are temporary block storage located on physically attached disks on the host computer, included with the hourly cost of your instance.

C. Instance Stores is a persistent storage system which offers volumes that are automatically replicated, included with the hourly cost of your instance.

D. Instance Stores is a block storage system which offers highly available block level storage volumes, included with the hourly cost of your instance.

14. Which of the following statements is true?

    A. On-Demand Instances can be used to alleviate traffic in a workload where many Reserved Instances are reading from a queue.

    B. Spot Blocks can be used to re-route traffic in a workload where many Reserved Instances are reading from a queue.

    C. Scheduled Instances can be used to alleviate traffic in a workload where many Reserved Instances are reading from a queue.

    D. Spot Instances can be used to alleviate traffic in a workload where many Reserved Instances are reading from a queue.

15. Which of the following EC2 instance type is storage optimized?

    A. T2

    B. C3

    C. I2

    D. X1

16. Which of the following statements is true?

    A. EIPs can be attached to the ENI's public IP addresses, and you can also attach one EIP with each public IP address.

    B. EIPs can be attached to the ENI's private IP addresses, but you cannot associate one EIP with each private IP address.

    C. EIPs cannot be attached to the ENI's private IP addresses.

    D. EIPs can be attached to the ENI's private IP addresses, and you can also attach one EIP with each private IP address.

17. What is an ENI?

    A. ENI is a virtual network interface that can be attached to an instance in a VPC.

    B. ENI is a point of interconnection between instances in a private or public network.

    C. ENI is an interface which can stipulate the signalling and management functions between two networks.

    D. ENI is an abstract virtualized representation which corresponds to instances in a default security group.

18. What is the best Instance type for Larger deployments of SAP, Microsoft SharePoint and other enterprise applications?

    A. R3

    B. I2

    C. T2

    D. D2

19. What is the characteristic of a D2 Instance Type?

    A. D2 Instance Type offers a balance of memory, compute and network resources.

B. D2 Instance Type offers lowest price per disk throughput performance.

C. D2 Instance Type offers lowest cost per GiB of RAM.

D. D2 Instance Type offers high IOPS at low costs.

20. Ann wants to configure the Reverse DNS record for an Elastic IP, how should Ann attempt this?

A. Reverse DNS record for an EIP can be configured by filling out a form and ensuring that a corresponding forward DNS record directing to the EIP address exists.

B. Reverse DNS record for an EIP can be configured by using EIP and Route 56 through the main AWS console.

C. Reverse DNS record for an EIP can be configured by filling out a form and using the allocated public IP address and mapping it to the server.

D. Reverse DNS record for an EIP can be configured by filling out a form and entering the static IP address for reverse DNS lookup.

21. What is a Default Security Group?

A. A VPC comes with a default security group which is attached to each EC2 instance and runs rules for outbound traffic.

B. A VPC comes with a default security group which is attached to each EC2 instance and runs rules for inbound and outbound traffic.

C. A VPC comes with a default security group which is attached to each EC2 instance that you launch, unless specified otherwise.

D. A VPC comes with a default security group which is attached to each EC2 instance and runs rules for inbound traffic.

22. Which of the following statements is true?

A. ENI Attributes: A primary public IP address 1 or more secondary public IP addresses

B. ENI Attributes: A primary private IP address 1 or more secondary private IP addresses

C. EIP Attributes: A primary private IP address 1 or more secondary private IP addresses

D. ENI Attributes: 1 or more primary private IP addresses A secondary private IP address

23. Which of the following statements is true?

A. Recommendation for launching new EC2 placement group: Launch instances randomly, as instances launched all at once result in 'insufficient capacity' error.

B. Recommendation for launching new EC2 placement group: Launch instances sequentially, adding instances later will be easy due to the order.

C. Recommendation for launching new EC2 placement group: Launch at once all instances you need, adding instances later may result in 'insufficient capacity' error.

D. Recommendation for launching new EC2 placement group: Launch instances periodically, as instances launched all at once result in 'insufficient capacity' error.

24. Which of the following statements is true?

A. Accumulation of CPU Credits by T2 Instances: T2.micro: 3 credits per hour T2.small: 6 credits per hour T2.medium: 9 credits per hour

B. Accumulation of CPU Credits by T2 Instances: T2.micro: 3 credits per hour T2.small: 6 credits per hour T2.medium: 12 credits per hour

C. Accumulation of CPU Credits by T2 Instances: T2.micro: 6 credits per hour T2.small: 12 credits per hour T2.medium: 18 credits per hour

D. Accumulation of CPU Credits by T2 Instances: T2.micro: 6 credits per hour T2.small: 12 credits per hour T2.medium: 24 credits per hour

25. What is the CPU Credit for an EC2 burstable instance type?

A. The performance of a full core for 30 seconds.

B. The performance of a full core for 120 seconds.

C. The performance of a full core for 60 seconds.

D. The performance of a full core for 240 seconds.

26. What is Bootstrapping?

A. Bootstrapping provides a script to be run on an instance at launch to initialize it with OS configurations and applications.

B. Bootstrapping provides a script to run a sequence of programs and manages OS, directories, and files.

C. Bootstrapping provides a script to start loading small programs one at a time.

D. Bootstrapping is a process which involves running of diagnostic programs to check configurations and resolves issues that come up.

27. Which of the following statements is true?

A. A placement group cannot span peered VPCs; and partial-bisection bandwidth might not be available between instances in peered VPCs in such a case.

B. A placement group can span peered VPCs. But, full-bisection bandwidth might not be available between instances in peered VPCs in such a case.

C. A placement group can span peered VPCs. But, partial-bisection bandwidth might not be available between instances in peered VPCs in such a case.

D. A placement group cannot span peered VPCs; and full-bisection bandwidth might not be available between instances in peered VPCs in such a case.

28. Amy wants to change an RI from one instance family (c1.4xlarge) to another (m1.xlarge), How should Amy attempt this?

A. An RI is attached to a specific instance family for the entire RI term, and can't be reassigned from one instance family to another, unless it is a Linux/UNIX RI.

B. RI that is attached to a specific instance family can be changed to another by submitting the request to Amazon via a form.

C. An RI is attached to a specific instance family for the entire RI term, and can't be reassigned from one instance family to another, unless it is a Windows RI.

D. RI that is attached to a specific instance family can be changed to another by switching over to an OS RI such as Linux or Windows RI

29. Sam wants to merge placement groups, how can Sam attempt this?

A. Placement groups cannot be merged, instead, create an AMI from the instance and launch a new instance from the AMI into a placement group.

B. Placement groups cannot be merged, instead, terminate the instances in one group, and relaunch the same instances into the other group.

C. Placement groups can be merged, by creating an AMI from the instance and passing it as a parameter to the placement group.

D. Placement groups can be merged, by specifying the instances as parameters to the calling group.

30. How can the Instance Metadata be obtained?

A. You can obtain Instance Metadata through a SOAP API.

B. You can obtain Instance Metadata through an HTTP call to a specific IP address.

C. You can obtain Instance Metadata through an API call by passing parameters of a pair of key-values.

D. You can obtain Instance Metadata through a REST API.

31. Which of the following is a characteristic of EC2 Placement Group?

A. Can span across AZs

B. Can be merged

C. Existing instances can be moved into placement groups

D. Cannot span across AZs

32. What is the best Instance type for NoSQL databases, Data Warehousing, Hadoop, and Cluster File Systems?

A. I2

B. D2

C. R3

D. T2

33. What is the best Instance type for Caching fleets, Small and mid-size databases, and data processing that needs extra memory?

A. I2

B. C3/C4

C. M3/M4

D. R3

34. Which of the following statements is true?

A. Instance Types that support Jumbo Frames (9001 MTU): Compute Optimized: R3 and CR1 Memory Optimized: HS1, HI1, D2 and I2

B. Instance Types that support Jumbo Frames (9001 MTU): Storage Optimized: R3 and CR1 Compute Optimized: HS1, HI1, D2 and I2

C. Instance Types that support Jumbo Frames (9001 MTU): General Purpose: R3 and CR1 Memory Optimized: HS1, HI1, D2 and I2

D. Instance Types that support Jumbo Frames (9001 MTU): Memory Optimized: R3 and CR1 Storage Optimized: HS1, HI1, D2 and I2

35. What are the capabilities of VM import/export?

A. EC2 allows you to import your existing virtual machines to AWS as instances, creating AMIs using paravirtual virtualization.

B. EC2 allows you to import your existing virtual machines to AWS as instances

or AMIs, and such imported instances can also be exported back to a virtual environment.

C. EC2 allows you to import your existing virtual machines to AWS as instances or AMIs and you can have up to 40 import image or snapshots tasks per region.

D. EC2 allows you to import VMs as AMI using GPT partitioned volumes.

36. What is Compute?

A. Compute is part of a web service that offers compute capacity in the cloud which is resizable.

B. Compute is wide range of the services offered with a high-level description that can leverage the complete solution for computing.

C. Compute is an instance which is acquired to balance memory and network resources for applications.

D. Compute is the amount of computational power needed to achieve your workload.

37. What is EBS-Backed in the context of an EC2 instance?

A. EBS-Backed: Where an instance store volume (created from a template saved in S3) is the root device for an instance launched from the AMI.

B. EBS-Backed: Where the backup process for a virtual machine (VM) is defined, and copies of the system state and application configurations are created.

C. EBS-Backed: Where an Amazon EBS volume (created from a snapshot) is the root device for an instance launched from the AMI.

D. EBS-Backed: Where the initial software state of an instance at the time of launch is defined and includes OS and configuration and initial state of patches.

38. Tom wants to move existing instances to placement groups, how should Tom attempt this?

A. Existing instances can be moved to placement groups, by creating an AMI from the instance and passing it as a parameter to the placement group.

B. Existing instances can be moved to placement groups, by specifying the instances as parameters to the calling group.

C. Existing instances can't be moved to placement groups, but you can create an AMI from the instance, and launch a new instance from the AMI into a placement group.

D. Existing instances can be moved to placement groups, by terminating the instances in one group and relaunching the same instances into the other group.

39. What is default maximum number of EC2 reservations per region?

A. 5 instance reservations/month per AZ

B. 10 instance reservations/month per AZ

C. 30 instance reservations/month per AZ

D. 20 instance reservations/month per AZ

40. How can you interpret the effect of Security Groups?

A. An instance that is a member of multiple security groups will have to implement the outbound traffic rules.

B. An instance that is a member of multiple security groups will have to implement the default security rules.

C. All the rules of all the security groups apply on an instance that is a member of several security groups.

D. An instance that is a member of multiple security groups will have to implement the inbound traffic rules.

41. What is Instance Store Backed in the context of an EC2 instance?

A. Instance Store Backed: Where the backup process for a virtual machine (VM) is defined, and copies of the system state and application configurations are created.

B. Instance Store Backed: Where the initial software state of an instance at the time of launch is defined and includes OS and configuration and initial state of patches.

C. Instance Store Backed: Where an instance store volume (created from a template saved in S3) is the root device for an instance launched from the AMI.

D. Instance Store Backed: Where an Amazon EBS volume (created from a snapshot) is the root device for an instance launched from the AMI.

42. What is the characteristic of an I2 Instance Type?

A. I2 Instance Type offers lowest price per disk throughput performance.

B. I2 Instance Type offers a balance of memory, compute and network resources.

C. I2 Instance Type offers high IOPS at low costs and provides high speed SSD-backed instance storage for very high random I/O performance.

D. I2 Instance Type offers lowest cost per GiB of RAM.

43. How can you access a newly launched Linux instance?

A. Linux: Use the private half of the key pair to decrypt the sequentially activated account owner password.

B. Linux: Use the private half of the key pair to connect to the instance via SSH.

C. Linux: Use the public half of the key pair to connect to the instance via TLS.

D. Linux: Use the private half of the key pair to decrypt the randomly initialized local administrator password.

44. Which of the following is a benefit of EC2 Placement Groups?

A. Low Price

B. 20 Gbps networking

C. High Latency

D. High throughput

45. Which of the following describes what the C3/C4 Instance Type is best suited for?

A. MPP data warehousing

B. Ad serving

C. Development environments

D. Data Warehousing

46. Which of the following is a feature of an On-Demand Instance?

A. Highest per hour cost

B. Idle compute capacities available on bid prices

C. Offer lower costs over the lifetime of reservation

D. Long-term compute needs

47. Which of the following describes what the G2 Instance Type is best suited for?

A. Ad serving

B. Caching fleets

C. Data Warehousing

D. Machine learning

48. Which of the following is an EC2 Metric available in CloudWatch?

A. Memory Utilization

B. CPU credits

C. CPU usage

D. Session checks

49. What is the characteristic of a C3/C4 Instance Type?

A. C3/C4 Instance Type offers high IOPS at low costs and provides high speed SSD-backed instance storage for very high random I/O performance.

B. C3/C4 Instance Type offers lowest cost per GiB of RAM.

C. C3/C4 Instance Type offers a balance of memory, compute and network resources, and offers the lowest price/compute performance and highest performing processors.

D. C3/C4 Instance Type offers lowest price per disk throughput performance.

50. What is the maximum number of RIs that can be purchased per AZ per month?

A. Up to 20 RIs can be purchased along with the EC2 APIs per month for every AZ. Any request for additional RIs will have to be submitted to Amazon via a form.

B. Up to 40 RIs can be purchased along with the EC2 APIs per month for every AZ. Any request for additional RIs will have to be submitted to Amazon via a form.

C. Up to 10 RIs can be purchased along with the EC2 APIs per month for every AZ. Any request for additional RIs will have to be submitted to Amazon via a form.

D. Up to 30 RIs can be purchased along with the EC2 APIs per month for every AZ. Any request for additional RIs will have to be submitted to Amazon via a form.

51. Which of the following is a benefit of Enhanced Networking?

A. Considerably higher PPS performance.

B. Provides high speed SSD-backed instance storage for very high random I/O performance.

C. Offers lowest price per disk throughput performance.

D. Offers high IOPS at low costs.

52. Emma wants to move an RI across a different AWS region, what should Emma know about moving RIs across regions?

A. RIs can be moved across different AWS regions, only if they are pre-approved.

B. RIs can be moved across different AWS regions, as the RI term extends flexibility.

C. RIs can be moved across different AWS regions, by associating them with another instance family in the other AWS region.

D. RIs cannot be moved across different AWS regions as they are associated with a particular region for the entire term.

53. Greg wants to apply RI capacity reservations to instances launched with an EC2 Placement Group, what should Greg know about RI Capacity Reservations?

A. Capacity reservations of reserved instances apply to spot instances within an EC2 placement group. They also apply for scheduled instances in an AZ.

B. Capacity reservations of reserved instances apply to

scheduled instances within an EC2 placement group. They also apply for spot instances in an AZ.

C. Capacity reservations of reserved instances do not apply to instances within an EC2 placement group. They apply for spot instances in an AZ.

D. Capacity reservations of reserved instances do not apply to instances within an EC2 placement group. They apply for on-demand instances in an AZ.

54. Which of the following is a feature of a Reserved Instance?

A. Need no up-front commitment

B. Highest per hour cost

C. Offer lower costs over the lifetime of reservation

D. Idle compute capacities available on bid prices

55. Amy wants to configure an EC2 security group to deny traffic, what should Amy know about configuring EC2 security groups?

A. An EC2 security group can only be configured to deny specific rules, and separate rules can be configured for inbound traffic only.

B. An EC2 security group can only be configured to allow default rules, and to deny specific rules.

C. An EC2 security group can only be configured to allow specific rules, not to deny any, and separate rules can be configured for outbound and inbound traffic.

D. An EC2 security group can be configured to allow and deny specific rules, and separate rules can be configured for outbound traffic only.

56. Lucy wants to use an existing ENI while creating new EC2 instance, how should Lucy attempt this?

A. You can use an existing ENI as the primary network interface to create a new instance by creating a management network and managing the instances.

B. You can use an existing ENI as the primary network interface to create a new instance by specifying the network interface.

C. You can use an existing ENI as the primary network interface to create a new instance by specifying an additional ENI and attaching it to the instance.

D. You can use an existing ENI as the primary network interface to create a new instance by specifying the ENI to be attached for both primary and additional ENIs.

# 4

# Virtual Private Cloud

1. What is a customer gateway (CGW)?

   A. A customer gateway is the anchor on your side of the connection, which uses BGP routing to make sure that all sites are reachable.

   B. A customer gateway is the anchor that links your data center to the cloud by creating VPN connections and configuring CloudHub.

   C. A customer gateway is the anchor on your side of the connection, which can restrict unwanted traffic by using pre-shared keys.

   D. A customer gateway is the anchor on your side of the connection, which can be software or a physical appliance.

2. Which of the following statements is true?

   A. Amazon does not allow you to change the size of an existing VPC, and you can terminate the VPC and create a new one with the desired CIDR block.

   B. Amazon does not authenticate the size of an existing VPC, and you can merge the VPC and create a new one with the desired CIDR block.

   C. Amazon allows you to change the size of an existing VPC, and you can initialize the VPC and create a new one with the desired CIDR block.

   D. Amazon does not merge the changed sizes of an existing VPC, and you can terminate the VPC and create a new one with the desired CIDR block.

3. Tim wants to connect multiple CGWs to a single VGW, what should Tim need to know about using CGWs with VGWs?

   A. Amazon VPC does not allow you to connect multiple CGWs to a single VGW, but allows connecting a single router to multiple VGWs.

   B. Amazon VPC does not allow you to connect multiple CGWs to a single VGW, or to connect a single router to multiple VGWs.

C. Amazon VPC allows you to connect multiple CGWs to a single VGW, but does not allow connecting a single router to multiple VGWs.

D. Amazon VPC allows you to connect multiple CGWs to a single VGW, or to connect a single router to multiple VGWs.

4. Which of the following statements is true?

A. EIP address is an AWS owned public IP address that can be automatically assigned to instances launched in a subnet.

B. Amazon VPC Public IP address is an AWS owned public IP address that can be automatically assigned to instances launched in a subnet.

C. Amazon VPC Public IP address is an AWS owned public IP address that can be manually assigned to instances using a subnet mask.

D. Amazon VPC Public IP address is a VPC owned public IP address that can be automatically routed to instances launched in a subnet.

5. What is the maximum number of VPN connections per VPC?

A. 30

B. 20

C. 10

D. 50

6. Which of the following statements is true?

A. VPC Primary Components: * IGWs * EIP addresses

B. VPC Optional Components: * IGWs * EIP addresses

C. VPC Optional Components: * IGWs * Route tables

D. VPC Optional Components: * Subnets * EIP addresses

7. Which of the following statements is true?

A. Endpoint is a VPC component that helps build a private connection between your S3 bucket and another DHCP Option set without needing access to the Internet.

B. Endpoint is a VPC component that helps build a private connection between your VPC and another AWS service (in the same region) without needing access over the Internet.

C. EIP is a VPC component that helps build a private connection between your VPC and another AWS service (in the same region) without needing access over the Internet.

D. Endpoint is an AWS-owned component that helps build a public connection between your VPC and another AWS service (in the same region) without needing access over the Internet.

8. What is a Subnet?

A. Subnets are segments of an Amazon VPC's IP address range, defined by CIDR blocks, where groups of isolated resources can be placed.

B. Subnets represent all machines which are at multiple geographic locations.

C. Subnets are part of an Amazon VPC strategy which uses multiple CIDR blocks and more than one logical sub-networks to acquire new network numbers via ISP.

D. Subnets are a 32-bit number which can differentiate Amazon VPC components of an IP address to connect to local networks via CIDR blocks.

9. What is a Private Subnet?

A. Private Subnet is a subnet that doesn't have a route to the IGW.

B. Private Subnet is a subnet that doesn't have a route to the IGW, but has the traffic routed via ISP.

C. Private Subnet is a subnet whose traffic is routed to an IGW.

D. Private Subnet is a subnet that doesn't have a route to the IGW, but has the traffic routed to a VPG.

10. What is a VPN CloudHub?

A. VPN CloudHub is an AWS service that uses the hub-and-spoke model to split the private networks using a CGW.

B. VPN CloudHub is an AWS service that lets you use the same BGP ASN to connect on-premise networks.

C. VPN CloudHub is an AWS service that lets you route between your on-premises networks using a VPG.

D. VPN CloudHub is an AWS service that allows remote sites to communicate between on-premises networks using an IPSec VPN.

11. What is a VPN-only Subnet?

A. VPN-only Subnet is a subnet that doesn't have a route to the IGW.

B. VPN-only Subnet is a subnet that doesn't have a route to the IGW, but has the traffic routed to a VPG.

C. VPN-only Subnet is a subnet that doesn't have a route to the IGW, but has the traffic routed via ISP.

D. VPN-only Subnet is a subnet whose traffic is routed to an IGW.

12. What are the characteristics of a Network ACL?

A. A Network ACL is applied on an object level and the traffic is stateless.

B. A Network ACL is applied on a subnet level and the traffic is stateless.

C. A Network ACL is applied on a subnet level and the traffic is stateful.

D. A Network ACL is applied on an instance level and the traffic is stateless.

13. What is Amazon VPC Peering?

A. Peering is a networking connection that, using a request/accept protocol, allows instances in 2 VPCs to communicate with each other like they are in the same network.

B. Peering is a networking connection that, using a request/poll protocol, allows routing of traffic between 2 VPCs to communicate, using public IP addresses.

C. Peering is a networking connection that, allows instances in 2 VPCs to exchange directly between ISPs without needing access to the Internet.

D. Peering is a networking connection that connects the VPC requestor and acceptor and helps them to communicate using their DHCP addresses.

14. What is the default maximum number of active peering connections per VPC?

A. Maximum no. of active peering connections per VPC: 15

B. Maximum no. of active peering connections per VPC: 5

C. Maximum no. of active peering connections per VPC: 35

D. Maximum no. of active peering connections per VPC: 50

15. Jenny wants to remove the Deny All rule at the bottom of an NACL rule list, what does Jenny need to know about the default deny all rule?

A. Every network ACL has a rule at the bottom of the rule list identified by an asterisk, which allows entry to a packet if it doesn't match any of the other rules.

B. Every network ACL has a rule at the bottom of the rule list identified by a Boolean, which terminates a packet if it doesn't match any of the other rules.

C. Every network ACL has a rule at the bottom of the rule list identified by an asterisk, which denies a packet if it doesn't match any of the other rules.

D. Every network ACL has a rule at the bottom of the rule list identified by a Boolean, which re-routes a packet to the parent if it doesn't match any of the other rules.

16. Which of the following statements is true?

A. Average size for a VPC: 28 (16 addresses)

B. Smallest possible size for a VPC: 38 (16 addresses)

C. Smallest possible size for a VPC: 28 (16 addresses)

D. Largest possible size for a VPC: 28 (16 addresses)

17. Which of the following statements is true?

A. ENI attributes: 1 public IP address A DHCP address A source/destination check flag

B. ENI attributes: 1 static IP address A MAC address A source/destination check flag

C. ENI attributes: 1 public IP address A MAC address A source/destination check flag

D. EIP attributes: 1 public IP address A MAC address A source/destination check flag

18. Which of the following statements is true?

A. Amazon VPC supports both multicast and broadcast.

B. Amazon VPC supports only multicast.

C. Amazon VPC does not support either multicast or broadcast.

D. Amazon VPC supports only broadcast.

19. Which of the following statements is true?

A. VPC Primary Components: * Subnets * EIP addresses

B. VPC Primary Components: * Subnets * Route tables

C. VPC Primary Components: * IGWs * Route tables

D. VPC Optional Components: * Subnets * Route tables

20. Which of the following statements is true?

A. The default network ACL of a VPC cannot be configured to let all inbound and outbound traffic to flow to and from each subnet.

B. The default network ACL of a VPC is configured to restrict all inbound and outbound traffic to flow to and from each subnet.

C. The default network ACL of a VPC is configured to let all inbound and outbound traffic to flow to and from each subnet.

D. The default network ACL of a VPC is configured to reroute all inbound and outbound traffic to flow to and from each subnet.

21. What is a DHCP Option set?

A. DHCP Option set is the component of Amazon VPC that helps you host name assignment to your own resources.

B. DHCP Option set is the component of DynamoDB that helps subnets to communicate with each other.

C. DHCP Option set is an EC3 component that helps to host your own private virtual network within the cloud.

D. DHCP Option set is the component of RDS that helps you host name assignment to your own resources.

22. Which of the following statements is true?

A. You cannot terminate access between VPC subnets using route tables.

B. You cannot modify access between VPC subnets using route tables.

C. You cannot restrict access between VPC subnets using route tables.

D. You cannot allow access between VPC subnets using route tables.

23. What is the default maximum number of VPC virtual private gateways per account per region?

A. Maximum no. of VPC virtual private gateways per account per region: 15

B. Maximum no. of VPC virtual private gateways per account per region: 5

C. Maximum no. of VPC virtual private gateways per account per region: 4

D. Maximum no. of VPC virtual private gateways per account per region: 6

24. Which of the following statements is true?

   A. You cannot use all the subnet addresses you assign to an IP as Amazon retains the first 5 and last 2 addresses of all subnets for IP networking uses.

   B. You cannot use all the IP addresses you assign to a subnet as Amazon retains the first 4 and last 1 addresses of all subnets for IP networking uses.

   C. You cannot use all the IP addresses you assign to a subnet as Amazon retains the first 5 and last 2 addresses of all subnets for IP networking uses.

   D. You cannot use all the subnet addresses you assign to an IP as Amazon retains the first 4 and last 1 addresses of all subnets for IP networking uses.

25. Which of the following statements is true?

   A. Maximum number of rules per security group: 500

   B. Maximum number of rules per security group: 50

   C. Maximum number of rules per security connection: 50

   D. Maximum number of rules per security group: 5

26. Meg wants to reference security groups across the connection in peered VPCs, what should Meg know about referencing security groups?

   A. Amazon VPC doesn't allow you to reference a security group from a peer VPC across the connection.

   B. Amazon VPC can reference a security group from a peer VPC across the connection by specifying the primary private IP address.

   C. Amazon VPC can reference a security group from a peer VPC across the connection by configuring rules.

   D. Amazon VPC can reference a security group from a peer VPC across the connection by creation of VPNs.

27. Which of the following statements is true?

   A. A NAT instance or a NAT gateway allows instances in public subnets to launch inbound traffic to the Internet, disabling download, but allowing outbound traffic.

   B. A NAT instance or a NAT gateway allows instances in private subnets to launch outbound traffic to the Internet, enabling download, but blocking inbound traffic.

   C. A NAT instance or a NAT gateway allows instances in public subnets to launch inbound traffic to the Internet, enabling download and outbound traffic.

   D. A NAT instance or a NAT gateway allows instances in private subnets to launch inbound traffic to the Internet, enabling download, but blocking outbound traffic.

28. Susan wants to modify the default Deny All rule, what should Susan need to know about modification of the Deny All rule?

   A. The default deny all rule cannot be removed but can be modified.

   B. The default deny all rule can be both removed and modified.

   C. The default deny all rule cannot be modified but can be removed.

   D. The default deny all rule cannot be removed or modified.

29. Susan wants to manually update route tables to route traffic across a VPC VPN link, what should Susan know about manually updating route tables?

   A. If Route Propagation is not turned on, you can manually update route tables to route traffic across a VPC VPN link.

   B. If Route Propagation is turned on, you cannot manually update route tables to route traffic across a VPC VPN link.

   C. If Route Propagation is not turned on, you can manually update route tables to route traffic across a VPC VPN link by choosing an AMI.

   D. If Route Propagation is not turned on, you can manually update route tables to route traffic across a VPC VPN link by specifying Static IP prefixes.

30. What is a Route Table?

   A. Route Table is a set of rules that helps determine the direction of network traffic, and lets EC2 instances within the same VPC, but different subnets to communicate.

   B. Route Table is a set of rules which are configured with a subnet mask of the interface and entered into the record sets of EC2 instances.

   C. Route Table is a set of rules that determines where record sets travel over an IP and lets EC3 instances within the same VPC communicate.

   D. Route Table is a set of rules that helps designate the zero-address in CIDR notation to effectively specify the network for same VPC to communicate.

31. Which of the following statements is true?

   A. Attributes of an ENI follow the EIP when it is attached/detached/reattached from and to instances.

   B. Attributes of an ENI follow the ENI when it is attached/detached/reattached from and to instances.

   C. Attributes of an ENI follow the ENI when it is terminated and new instances are created.

   D. Attributes of an ENI follow the DHCP when it is authenticated from and to instances.

# 5

# Load Balancing and Scaling

1. Which of the following is an ELB protocol that supports the Proxy Protocol?

   A. TLS

   B. HTTPS

   C. UDP

   D. TCP

2. Which of the following is an aspect that ELB allows to configure of the load balancer?

   A. Proxy Protocol

   B. Health checks

   C. Stick sessions

   D. Cross-zone load balancing

3. How can you get a history of ELB API calls?

   A. You cannot get a history of the API calls made on your account.

   B. You can get a history of the API calls made on your account by turning on Cloud-Sense in your AWS Management Console.

   C. You can get a history of the API calls made on your account by turning on Cloud-Watch in your AWS Management Console.

   D. You can get a history of the API calls made on your account by turning on Cloud-Trail in your AWS Management Console.

4. What is the characteristic of an Internal load balancer in ELB?

   A. Internal load balancer balances load between the tiers of a multi-tier application. E.g. Routes traffic to EC2 instances in VPCs with private subnets.

   B. Internal load balancer encrypts data between clients who initiate HTTPS sessions and a load balancer.

   C. Internal load balancer encrypts data between clients who initiate SSH sessions and a load balancer.

   D. Internal load balancer in ELB takes requests from clients over the Internet, and allocates them to EC2 instances registered with the load balancer.

5. Which of the following statements is true?

A. Benefits of ELB Cross-Zone Load Balancing: Enhances the network's capacity to withstand the loss of one or more front-end instances.

B. Benefits of ELB Cross-Zone Load Balancing: Enhances an EC2 instance's capacity to return the unhealthy back-end instances.

C. Benefits of ELB Cross-Zone Load Balancing: Enhances an application's capacity to withstand the loss of one or more back-end instances.

D. Benefits of ELB Health Check: Enhances an application's capacity to withstand the loss of one or more back-end instances.

6. Which of the following statements is true?

A. The Amazon CloudTrail log data is stored for 10 years for you to retrieve and use.

B. The Amazon CloudWatch log data is stored for 20 years for you to retrieve and use.

C. The Amazon CloudWatch log data is stored for 5 years for you to retrieve and use.

D. The Amazon CloudWatch log data is stored for 10 years for you to retrieve and use.

7. What is Elastic Load Balancing?

A. Elastic Load Balancing is a highly available AWS compute service that achieves failover whenever there is failure.

B. Elastic Load Balancing is a highly available AWS compute service that can manually be scaled to meet the requests of inbound traffic.

C. Elastic Load Balancing is a highly available AWS compute service that enables greater fault tolerance levels by distributing traffic across a group of EC2 instances in one or multiple AZs.

D. Elastic Load Balancing is a highly available AWS compute service that provides load balancing capacity by routing traffic to EC3 instances in same AWS regions.

8. Which of the following statements is true?

A. If EC3 instances are healthy, the ELB Health Check status returns as InService, and if not, it returns as OutOfService.

B. If EC2 instances are healthy, the ELB Health Check status returns as ServiceTrue, and if not, it returns as ServiceFalse.

C. If EC2 instances are healthy, the ELB Health Check status returns as InService, and if not, it returns as OutOfService.

D. If EC3 instances are healthy, the ELB Health Check status returns as InService, and if not, it returns as NotInService.

9. What is the characteristic of an Internet-facing load balancer in ELB?

A. Internet-facing load balancer encrypts data between clients who initiate SSH sessions and a load balancer.

B. Internet-facing load balancer balances load between the tiers of a multi-tier application. E.g. Routes traffic to EC2 instances in VPCs with private subnets.

C. Internet-facing load balancer encrypts data between clients who initiate HTTPS sessions and a load balancer.

D. Internet-facing load balancer in ELB takes requests from clients over the Internet, and allocates them to EC2 instances registered with the load balancer.

10. What is a common use case for Amazon CloudWatch?

A. In an application tier, you can decide when to add or remove EC2 instances by monitoring disk utilization using CloudWatch.

B. In an application tier, you can decide when to add or remove EC2 instances by monitoring CPU utilization using CloudWatch.

C. In an application tier, you can decide when to add or remove EC3 instances by monitoring memory utilization using CloudWatch.

D. In an application tier, you can decide when to add or remove EC3 instances by monitoring processor idle time using CloudWatch.

11. Which of the following is a use case for Amazon CloudWatch?

A. Auto Scaling can be used to: Streamline costs by decreasing the number of running EC3 instances during troughs/demand dulls.

B. Auto Scaling can be used to: Minimize costs by decreasing the number of running EC2 instances during troughs/demand dulls.

C. Auto Scaling can be used to: Minimize costs by decreasing the number of existing EC2 instances during troughs/demand dulls.

D. Auto Scaling can be used to: Minimize costs by terminating the number of running EC2 instances during troughs/demand dulls.

12. Which of the following is a step to create an SSL certificate for ELB?

A. Get the certificate signed by an object owner

B. Create an RSA private key and a CSR

C. Get the certificate signed by an account owner

D. Create a RapidSSL private key and a CSR

13. What is Amazon CloudWatch?

A. Amazon CloudWatch is a service that records AWS API calls for your AWS account by passing parameters as per client defined rules.

B. Amazon CloudWatch is a tool that helps to speed up the distribution of web content as per client defined rules.

C. Amazon CloudWatch is a tool that helps to integrate search capabilities into other applications based on client defined rules.

D. Amazon CloudWatch is a tool that helps monitor resources by collecting and tracking metrics, creating notification alarms, and modifying monitored resources as per client defined rules.

14. Which of the following statements is true?

A. For back-end connections: Configured with a protocol and a port; client to load balancer.

B. For front-end connections: Configured with a protocol and a network connection; client to HTTPS session.

C. For front-end connections: Configured with a protocol and a port; client to load balancer.

D. For front-end connections: Configured with a protocol and a port; load balancer to back-end instance.

15. How does the Amazon CloudWatch Log work?

A. How it works: Once you install a CloudWatch Log Agent on your EC2 instance, it performs health checks on log information and sends it back to CloudWatch.

B. How it works: Once you install a CloudWatch Log Agent on your EC3 instance, it publishes log rules and sends it back to CloudWatch.

C. How it works: Once you install a CloudWatch Log Agent on your EC2 instance, it records log information and stores it in DynamoDB.

D. How it works: Once you install a CloudWatch Log Agent on your EC2 instance, it collects log information and sends it back to CloudWatch.

16. Which of the following is a type of Amazon CloudWatch monitoring?

A. Informative

B. Secondary

C. Primary

D. Basic

17. Tom wants to same multiple SSL certificates on an ELB, what should Tom know about storing SSL certificates on ELB?

A. You cannot save more than one SSL certificate on an ELB.

B. You can save more than one SSL certificate on an ELB by using front-end listeners.

C. You can save more than one SSL certificate on an ELB by turning on CloudTrail.

D. You can save more than one SSL certificate on an ELB.

18. Which of the following statements is true?

A. You can use a DV certificate to terminate SSL on an ELB.

B. You can use an EV certificate to terminate SSL on an ELB.

C. You can use a self-signed certificate to terminate SSL on an ELB.

D. You can use an SSL Server certificate to terminate SSL on an ELB.

19. Which of the following TCP port is supported for ELB?

   A. Port 25
   B. Port 22
   C. Port 53
   D. Port 23

20. What is Auto Scaling?

   A. Auto Scaling is an AWS service that can distribute incoming and outgoing traffic using ELB.
   B. Auto Scaling is an AWS service that lets service providers validate PCI DSS compliance and includes automatic routing of traffic.
   C. Auto Scaling is an AWS service that lets customers specify criteria through a user-interface passing parameter named Action to build scaling requests.
   D. Auto Scaling is an AWS service that lets customers define criteria based on which their Amazon EC2 capacity can be automatically scaled in or out.

21. Which of the following is a valid status for any instance in an ELB?

   A. InService
   B. NotKnown
   C. NotInService
   D. NotUnknown

22. Charlie wants to use ELB cross-zone load balancing, how much should Charlie pay for the inter-zone transfer between the load balancer and back-end instances?

   A. If you have enabled cross-zone load balancing, the charges are a per month model for the inter-zone data transfer between back-end instances and the load balancer nodes.
   B. If you have enabled cross-zone load balancing, there are no extra charges for inter-zone data transfer between back-end instances and the load balancer nodes.
   C. If you have enabled cross-zone load balancing, the charges are hourly for the inter-zone data transfer between back-end instances and the load balancer nodes.
   D. If you have enabled cross-zone load balancing, the charges are per GB for the inter-zone data transfer between back-end instances and the load balancer nodes.

23. Which of the following is a type of load balancer in ELB?

   A. FTP-facing load balancer
   B. SSH load balancer
   C. Internal load balancer
   D. DHCP load balancer

24. What are the characteristics of Amazon CloudWatch Detailed monitoring?

   A. Detailed monitoring: Default; Free; Sends data points for a limited number of pre selected metrics to CloudWatch (every 5 minutes).

B. Detailed monitoring: Default; Free; Sends data points for an unlimited number of pre selected metrics to CloudWatch (every 10 minutes).

C. Detailed monitoring: Must be enabled; Charged; Sends data points every minute; Allows data aggregation.

D. Detailed monitoring: Must be enabled; Charged; Sends data points every 10 minute; Allows data integration.

25. What is the default ELB timeout for client and back-end connections?

A. 120 seconds

B. 90 seconds

C. 30 seconds

D. 60 seconds

26. Which of the following statements is true?

A. For back-end connections: Configured with an internet-facing load balancer to back-end instance.

B. For back-end connections: Configured with a protocol and a port; load balancer to back-end instance.

C. For back-end connections: Configured with AZs and a port; load balancer to EC3 instance.

D. For back-end connections: Configured with a protocol and a port; client to load balancer.

27. Which of the following is an EC2 Metric available in CloudWatch?

A. Memory Utilization

B. CPU credits

C. CPU usage

D. Session checks

28. What is the characteristic of an HTTPS load balancer in ELB?

A. HTTPS load balancer in ELB takes requests from clients over the Internet, and allocates them to EC2 instances registered with the load balancer.

B. HTTPS load balancer encrypts data between clients who initiate HTTPS sessions and a load balancer.

C. HTTPS load balancer balances load between the tiers of a multi-tier application. E.g. Routes traffic to EC2 instances in VPCs with private subnets.

D. HTTPS load balancer encrypts data between clients who initiate SSH sessions and a load balancer.

29. Bill wants to check the status of a particular instance in an ELB, what should Bill know about checking the status of a specific instance in an ELB?

A. ELB can check the status of a particular instance which has the cross-zone load balancing enabled.

B. ELB does not allow you to check the status of a particular instance.

C. ELB allows you to check the status of a particular instance.

D. ELB can check the status of a particular instance which is InService.

30. Which of the following is a plan which can help control Auto Scaling performance?

    A. Maintain Dynamic Instant Levels

    B. Instant Scaling

    C. Root Scaling

    D. Maintain Current Instant Levels

# 6

# Identity and Access Management

1. Which of the following statements is true?

   A. Authorization is the process of defining group memberships of users, and determining the actions a user can and cannot carry out by associating them with policies.

   B. Authorization is the process of creating long-term credentials for principals thereby determining the actions a principal can and cannot carry out by associating them with policies.

   C. Authorization is the process of creating principals, and defining their roles by associating them with policies.

   D. Authorization is the process where IAM manages the access of individual principals, and determines the actions a principal can and cannot carry out by associating them with policies.

2. Amy is searching for an additional layer of security for sensitive API calls, what do you suggest Amy should use?

   A. Use long-term credentials for an additional layer of security for sensitive API calls.

   B. Use temporary security credentials for an additional layer of security for sensitive API calls.

   C. Use an account owner's credentials for an additional layer of security for sensitive API calls.

   D. Use MFA for an additional layer of security for sensitive API calls.

3. Which of the following statements is true?

   A. EC2 Instance Profile is a container for IAM users which can be used to associate IAM groups to an EC2 instance at instance start-up.

   B. EC2 Instance Profile is an identifier for IAM groups which can be used to associate users to an EC2 instance at instance start-up.

   C. EC2 Instance Profile is an identifier for IAM roles which can be used to find out unique roles of an EC2 instance at instance start-up.

D. EC2 Instance Profile is a container for IAM roles which can be used to associate roles to an EC2 instance at instance start-up.

4. Which of the following statements is true?

   A. Policy Components are: * Effect * Service * Action

   B. Policy Components are: * Effect * Service * Operations

   C. Policy Components are: * Effect * Service * Tokens

   D. Policy Components are: * Rotating Keys * Service * Action

5. What is an Identity Broker in the context of an IAM identity federation?

   A. Identity Broker is an application that helps to integrate external identity providers.

   B. Identity Broker is the component that requests for new credentials before the expiry of the temporary security credentials.

   C. Identity Broker is a custom-developed application that enables users to access the AWS Management Console by authenticating against the local identity store.

   D. Identity Broker is a component that runs real-time to integrate with IAM using SAML.

6. Eva wants to switch to an IAM role by attempting to use an account owner's credentials, how do you suggest Eva switch to an IAM role?

   A. To switch to an IAM Role use AWS MFA devices.

   B. To switch to an IAM Role use Temporary security credentials or IAM user credentials.

   C. To switch to an IAM Role use SAML.

   D. To switch to an IAM Role use an Account owner's credentials.

7. What is an Identity Provider?

   A. Identity Provider is the entity that allows IAM Users to be added to or removed from a group.

   B. Identity Provider is the entity that manages and grants permissions to users outside of AWS to access and use AWS resources.

   C. Identity Provider is the entity which allows an authenticated actor to assume a role, in order to access AWS cloud services for a specified period.

   D. Identity Provider is the entity that enables granular level control over the people and applications that can access an AWS account.

8. Which of the following statements is true?

   A. IAM is an operating system identity management where the users can access an AWS account through the operating system console.

   B. IAM enables granular level control over the data and applications in an AWS account as defined by the root user.

C. IAM enables granular level control over the people and applications that can access an AWS account.

D. IAM enables operational level control over the people and applications that can access an AWS account through the CLI.

9. Which of the following best describes a way of handling multiple permissions?

A. Action not implicitly allowed by a policy is denied.

B. Action explicitly allowed by a policy is denied.

C. Action not explicitly allowed by a policy is denied.

D. Action explicitly deactivated by a policy is deleted.

10. What is a Temporary Security Token?

A. Temporary Security Token is a token that is identical to a wireless network key and is configured only on the expiry of the temporary security credentials.

B. Temporary Security Token is a token that is programmatically generated on request for new credentials and is-sued on expiry of the temporary security credentials.

C. Temporary Security Token is a token that is obtained by AWS STS and the credentials include an access key, a public key, and a session token.

D. Temporary Security Token is a token issued by the AWS STS to an authenticated actor who assumes a role, in order to access AWS cloud services for a specified period.

11. Which of the following is the maximum of IAM Users per AWS account?

A. 1500

B. 2500

C. 5000

D. 5500

12. Sam is exploring why there is an immediate access denial for any application running on an EC2 instance that is attached to an IAM role, what is Sam attempting?

A. Deletion of the administrator's personal IAM account.

B. Revoking of IAM Roles when attached to EC2 instances.

C. IAM Role attached to EC2 instances not having requisite permissions.

D. Deletion of IAM Roles when attached to EC2 instances.

13. Which of the following statements is true?

A. Groups can directly access AWS by making requests to the power user.

B. Groups can directly access AWS as they have the requisite security credentials of their own.

C. Groups cannot directly access AWS as they do not have security credentials of their own.

D. Groups can indirectly access AWS by making requests to the power user.

14. S3 buckets represent what kind of services?

A. Services supporting authentication of IAM User accounts.

B. Services supporting AWS actions.

C. Services supporting AWS resources.

D. Services supporting resource-based IAM policies.

15. Which of the following is an entity to which an IAM policy can be assigned?

A. AWS MFA device

B. Role

C. AWS Federation Endpoint

D. SAML 2.0 IdP

16. Which of the following statements is true?

A. An IAM group can send requests for the granting of its own IAM role to a power user who can assign policies to such roles.

B. An IAM user cannot be granted its own IAM role as there is no option of assigning policies to such roles.

C. An IAM group cannot be granted its own IAM role as there is no option of assigning policies to such roles.

D. An IAM group can grant its own IAM role as there are multiple options for assigning policies to such roles.

17. Which of the following statements is true?

A. Explicit policies are evaluated and an explicit request is allowed to override the enforcement code.

B. All policies are evaluated and by default, all requests that are made are allowed.

C. All policies are evaluated and an explicit request is allowed to override the enforcement code.

D. All policies are evaluated and by default, all requests that are made are denied.

18. Which of the following best describes what rotation of keys can secure?

A. IAM User Accounts

B. AWS Resources

C. IAM Devices

D. AWS Actions

19. Which of the following statements is true?

A. IAM Group is an account that can be authenticated using IAM, created for group of people to access an AWS account.

B. Federated User is a constant account that can be controlled using IAM, created for people or applications to access an AWS account.

C. IAM Account owner is a permanent account that can be created using IAM, for power users to access an AWS account.

D. IAM User is a constant account that can be controlled using IAM, created for people or applications to access an AWS account.

20. What is an Access Key and Session Token used to authenticate?

A. IAM Power User

B. AWS Actions

C. IAM Device

D. IAM principal

21. Which of the following best describes the number of access keys that can be assigned to an IAM user?

A. 10

B. 20

C. 3

D. 2

22. Which of the following best describes the use of conditions in AWS?

A. Conditions provide security as they help compute time intervals between events.

B. Conditions provide security to IAM roles by defining the client IP address ranges.

C. Conditions help to process events in reduced time.

D. Conditions provide security to IAM user accounts by restricting client IP address ranges.

23. Which of the following statements is true?

A. AWS MFA uses an authentication device that generates random, single-use, six-digit codes.

B. AWS MFA uses an authentication algorithm that generates a true random, single-use, eight-digit codes.

C. AWS MFA uses an authentication device that generates random, multi-use, three-digit codes.

D. AWS MFA uses an authentication application that generates random, multi-use, eight-digit codes.

24. Which of the following best describes a step performed by an Identity Broker?

A. Creates an IAM role that only allows a user to create EC2 instances in a specific VPC.

B. Calls the AWS federation endpoint.

C. Calls AWS federation endpoint to get a sign in token using temporary credentials.

D. Changes the IAM Role on a Running Instance.

25. Which of the following best describes a step in a key rotation?

A. Decrypt the old key.

B. Deactivate the temporary key.

C. Initialize the new key with values.

D. Configure all applications to use the new key.

26. Which of the following is a step to create an SSO URL for Federated Users?

A. Constructing a URL using the token from the federation endpoint.

B. Using the Access Control Policies.

C. Using an Account owner's credentials.

D. Using AWS MFA devices.

27. Which of the following statements is true?

A. The three types of IAM principals are: * Root Users * IAM Users * Roles

B. The three types of IAM principals are: * Root Users * AWS Users * Roles

C. The three types of IAM principals are: * Root Users * Super Users * Roles

D. The three types of IAM principals are: * Root Users * IAM Users * Bucket Resources

28. Which of the following statements is true?

A. You cannot change the permissions of an IAM Group on a Running Instance.

B. You can change the permissions of an IAM User on a Running Instance.

C. You cannot change the IAM Role on a Running Instance.

D. You can change the IAM Role on a Running Instance.

29. What is a Key Rotation?

A. Key Rotation is the process of creating new enforcement code keys for IAM groups to reduce access vulnerabilities and allow two active keys to function at a time.

B. Key Rotation is the process of regularly creating new access keys for IAM users in order to reduce security risks, where IAM allows two active keys to function at a time.

C. Key Rotation is the process of creating temporary security credentials for IAM users to reduce security risks and allow a pair of active credentials to work together.

D. Key Rotation is the process of creating authentication code keys for IAM roles to reduce redundancies, where IAM allows two active keys to function at a time.

30. Which of the following statements is true?

A. Policies can be attached to IAM account owners directly or to IAM roles.

B. Policies can be attached to IAM users directly or to an IAM group that the user is a member of.

C. Policies can be attached to IAM roles directly or to an IAM user.

D. Policies can be attached to IAM users directly or to an IAM group that the account owner assigns.

31. How is a Root User defined?

A. Root User is the single sign-in principal associated with the actual AWS account with complete access which cannot be in any way restricted.

B. Root user is the initial principal with the UID of zero who can make system-wide changes.

C. Root User is the single sign-in principal who can access web service APIs and is responsible for the maintenance of the AWS account.

D. Root User is the principal who can control constant accounts using IAM, created for people or applications to access an AWS account.

32. Which of the following describes a component of an IAM Request Context?

A. LDAP-based identity store

B. Functional data

C. Secret access key

D. Calling principal

33. Which of the following describes how MFA works in AWS?

A. MFA is an authentication process that uses a password (a knowledge factor) and a key generated through a mathematical algorithm to authenticate an AWS account.

B. MFA is an authentication process that has a one-step verification to authenticate an AWS account.

C. MFA is a process that is password-based and relies on the diligence of an account owner to authenticate an AWS account.

D. MFA is an authentication process that uses both a password (something you know) and a device generated OTP (something you have) to authenticate an AWS account.

34. Which of the following best describes a step performed by an Identity Broker?

A. Changes the IAM Role on a Running Instance.

B. Calls the AWS federation endpoint.

C. Creates an IAM role that only allows a user to create EC2 instances in a specific VPC.

D. Calls AWS STS to get user's temporary security credentials and permissions information.

35. Which of the following best describes a characteristic of Delegation?

A. Delegation is the process of granting of access rights to users outside of AWS.

B. Delegation is the process of granting of access rights for one AWS account to users in another AWS account.

C. Delegation enables granular level control over the people and applications that can access an AWS account.

D. Delegation is the process of allowing IAM Users to be added to or removed from a group.

36. Which of the following best describes an IAM group characteristic?

A. IAM groups can contain multiple groups.

B. IAM Groups can be nested.

C. Permissions can be granted to groups using access control policies.

D. Permissions can be granted to groups by the root user.

37. What is an IAM External ID?

A. IAM External ID is an identifier that consolidates identities from external IdPs.

B. IAM External ID is an identifier that allows calls to AWS STS to get user's temporary security credentials and permissions information.

C. IAM External ID is an identifier that can be granted to a third party in order for them to assume a role and access an AWS account.

D. IAM External ID is a unique key for IAM roles which can be used to associate roles to an EC2 instance at instance start-up.

38. Meg wants to access AWS resources and call MFA-protected APIs, how should Meg attempt this?

    A. To access AWS resources and call MFA-protected APIs, Pass MFA authentication code in the AWS STS API requests using secure stored versions.

    B. To access AWS resources and call MFA-protected APIs, Pass optional MFA parameters in the AWS STS API requests using temporary credentials.

    C. To access AWS resources and call MFA-protected APIs, Pass optional enforcement codes in the AWS STS API requests using long-term credentials.

    D. To access AWS resources and call MFA-protected APIs, pass parameters that are validated by account owners.

39. Which of the following statements is true?

    A. IAM Root User common use case includes assigning privileges to an Amazon EC2 instance that can be assumed by the applications running on the particular instance.

B. IAM Users common use case includes assigning privileges to an Amazon EC2 instance that can be assumed by the applications running on the particular instance.

C. IAM roles common use case includes assigning privileges to an Amazon EC2 instance that can be extended to the applications running on multi-threaded instances.

D. IAM roles common use case includes assigning privileges to an Amazon EC2 instance that can be assumed by the applications running on the particular instance.

40. Ken is working with the GetFederatedSession API that is MFA-protected and wants to pass MFA parameters, what should Ken know about API access for federated users?

    A. MFA-protected API access works for federated users and the GetFederatedSession API accepts MFA parameters, adding an extra security level.

    B. MFA-protected API access does not work for federated users as the GetFederatedSession API does not accept MFA parameters.

    C. MFA-protected API access is supported for federated users through the GetFederatedSession API which accepts info and context as parameters.

    D. MFA-protected API access does not work for unauthenticated IAM users as the GetFederatedSession API does not accept MFA parameters.

41. Which of the following best describes the characteristics of IAM Users geography?

    A. IAM Users are regionally defined entities and are bound by the geographic region which they belong to, in order to access resources.

    B. IAM Users follow a clustered model which allows access to AWS resources which are geographically close to them.

    C. IAM Users are global entities, and have unrestricted user privileges when it comes to accessing AWS services.

    D. IAM Users are global entities that do not need a geographic region to be specified while defining user permissions.

42. Which of the following best describes an IAM user characteristic?

    A. One user can be added to multiple groups.

    B. To add one user to multiple groups the root user needs to set permissions.

    C. One User can be added to a single group only.

    D. Users need to be authorized during creation to be added to multiple groups.

43. Tia wants to protect access to specific AWS resources, how can Tia attempt this?

    A. Use MFA to protect access to specific AWS resources.

    B. Use long-term credentials to protect access to specific AWS resources.

    C. Use temporary security credentials to protect access to specific AWS resources.

    D. Use account owner's credentials to protect access to specific AWS resources.

44. Which of the following statements is true?

    A. AWS Federation Endpoint can be used to allow federated users to access AWS APIs.

    B. SAML can be used to allow external users to access AWS APIs.

    C. SAML can be used to allow federated users to access AWS APIs.

    D. SAML can be used to allow federated users to access AWS MFA devices.

45. Which of the following is a common use case for an IAM role?

    A. Root-account access.

    B. Consolidating identities from external IdPs.

    C. Consolidating identities from internal IdPs.

    D. Multi-user access.

46. Which of the following statements is true?

    A. MFA authentication enforces restrictions to IAM policies which are set by the account owner.

    B. MFA authentication is enforced by using temporary credentials related to IAM policies.

C. MFA authentication is enforced by using long-term credentials related to IAM policies.

D. MFA authentication is enforced by attaching MFA related restrictions to IAM policies.

47. Which of the following statements is true?

    A. There is an option of setting specific usage quota for individual IAM users; usage limits on the entire AWS account does not apply.

    B. There is no option of setting specific usage quota for entire AWS account; usage limits on individual IAM user account apply.

    C. There is no option of setting specific usage quota for individual IAM users; usage limits on the entire AWS account apply.

    D. There is no option of setting specific account creation quota for individual IAM users; usage patterns from the entire AWS account are analyzed.

# 7

# Database Services

1. Which of the following is a benefit of Amazon Redshift?

   A. Can configure high levels of provisioned read and write capacity.

   B. Creates tables in high speed to scale to an unlimited number of items.

   C. Supports both simple and complex data types (E.g. String and Number and List and Map, respectively).

   D. Fast query performance through distributing records using columnar storage and parallelizing query execution across several compute nodes.

2. Which of the following is a use of the DynamoDB Cross regional table Copy AWS data pipeline?

   A. Helps in disaster recovery during region failure or data loss.

   B. Helps in BCP during region failure or data loss.

   C. Takes partial data backups.

   D. Supports applications within same regions by archiving DynamoDB data.

3. Ann wants to configure Redshift to copy snapshots across regions, how should Ann attempt this?

   A. Snapshots of Redshift clusters can be configured to be automatically copied to another AWS region, but it can only be copied to one destination region at a time.

   B. Snapshots of Redshift clusters can be configured to be automatically copied to another AWS region, and it can be copied to multiple destination regions at a time.

   C. Snapshots of Redshift clusters cannot be configured to be automatically copied to another AWS region, but it can be copied to one destination region at a time manually.

   D. Snapshots of Redshift clusters cannot be configured to be automatically copied to another AWS region.

4. Which of the following is a best practice to improve DynamoDB performance?

A. Link query attributes into multiple LSI.

B. Relocate least frequently accessed items into a different AWS region with lesser IOPS.

C. Make sure the keys are evenly allocated across partitions.

D. Distribute tables by classification frequency to reduce query IOPS.

5. Which of the following is a benefit of Amazon Redshift?

A. Supports large databases by allowing scaling up or down of clusters using magnetic disk storage or SSD.

B. Supports both simple and complex data types (E.g. String and Number and List and Map, respectively).

C. Creates tables in high speed to scale to an unlimited number of items.

D. Can configure high levels of provisioned read and write capacity.

6. Which of the following is a condition that can trigger an automated failover of a Multi-AZ RDS Instance?

A. Change in the instance's storage type.

B. Manual failover initiated via the 'Standby with Failover' API call.

C. Manual failover initiated via the 'Terminate with Failover' API call.

D. Change in the instance's process type.

7. How can the disabling/enabling encryption on existing Redshift Clusters be attempted?

A. To disable/enable encryption on existing Redshift Clusters, copy data from the cluster and move it to a new cluster with the default encryption setting.

B. To disable/enable encryption on existing Redshift Clusters, unload data from the cluster and reload it to a new cluster with a preferred encryption setting.

C. To disable/enable encryption on existing Redshift Clusters, copy data from the cluster and move it to a new cluster with a preferred encryption setting.

D. To disable/enable encryption on existing Redshift Clusters, copy data from the cluster and move it to another cluster with a preferred encryption setting.

8. What is Amazon DynamoDB?

A. Amazon DynamoDB is a high-speed, completely managed petabyte-scale cloud based data warehouse service optimized for highly efficient analysis and reporting of very large datasets.

B. Amazon DynamoDB is a completely managed database service that simplifies administration and operations for NoSQL databases providing low-latency and high scalability performance.

C. Amazon DynamoDB is a high latency, completely managed scalable cloud based data mining service optimized for highly efficient applications and resources of clients.

D. Amazon DynamoDB is a service that streamlines the setup, operations, and scaling of a relational database on AWS, making it easy for customers to focus on application and schema.

9. What is the default maximum number of RDS read replicas per master database?

A. 100

B. 40

C. 50

D. 5

10. Which of the following are options which are NOT available of RDS?

A. Use RDS CLI or RDS API.

B. Encrypt databases using keys through KMS.

C. Provision Multi-AZ database instance.

D. Accessing OS.

11. Which of the following is a best practice to improve DynamoDB performance?

A. Relocate least frequently accessed items into a different AWS region with lesser IOPS.

B. Link query attributes into multiple LSI.

C. Spread items across a fixed number of shards and attach a random shard identifier to shard writes of very hot tables.

D. Distribute tables by classification frequency to reduce query IOPS.

12. Which of the following is a format of a NoSQL Database?

A. WebM stores

B. FLAC stores

C. Document databases

D. PNG files

13. Which of the following is an allowable RDS Storage Type?

A. Provisioned IOPS Storage

B. Special Purpose (SSD) Storage

C. Queue IOPS Storage

D. Latency (Standard) Storage

14. What is a Relational Database?

A. Relational Database is the most commonly used database type that is organized like a tree structure with records connected to one another as links.

B. Relational Database is the most commonly used database type that offers a logical structure where the data can be stored, manipulated, and organized and looks like a graph.

C. Relational Database is the most commonly used database type that offers a common interface where users can read/write from the database through queries/commands written using SQL.

D. Relational Database is the most commonly used database type which is like an upside-down tree structure with multiple member records or files linked to multiple owner files.

15. Guy wants to manually initiate a failover for an RDS instance, how should Guy attempt this?

   A. RDS automatically fails over an instance in many failure conditions, and a manual failover can be done during launch of instance via an API call or the AWS Management Console.

   B. RDS automatically fails over an instance in many failure conditions, and a manual failover can be done during the modification of instance via an API call or the AWS Management Console.

   C. RDS automatically fails over an instance in many failure conditions, and a manual failover can be done during the termination of instance via an API call or the AWS Management Console.

   D. RDS automatically fails over an instance in many failure conditions, and a manual failover can be done during reboot via an API call or the AWS Management Console.

16. Lou wants to use Standby Replicas for 'read traffic', what should Lou know about using standby replicas for 'read traffic'?

   A. You cannot use Standby Replicas to serve 'Read Traffic' in RDS Multi-AZ deployments or use a Read Replica.

   B. You cannot use Standby Replicas to serve 'Read Traf-

fic' in RDS Multi-AZ deployments, but you will have to use a Read Replica.

   C. You can use Standby Replicas to serve 'Read Traffic' in RDS Multi-AZ deployments.

   D. You can use Standby Replicas to serve 'Read Traffic' in RDS Multi-AZ deployments, but and you can use a Read Replica.

17. Which of the following statements is true?

   A. You can copy an automated RDS DB snapshot to create a manual snapshot in the same AWS region.

   B. You cannot copy an automated RDS DB snapshot to create a manual snapshot in the same AWS region.

   C. You can copy a manual RDS DB snapshot to create an automated snapshot in the same AWS region.

   D. You cannot copy a manual RDS DB snapshot to create an automated snapshot in the same AWS region.

18. Tom wants to know whether restoring an RDS snapshot/point-in-time recovery have a new endpoint, what should Tom know about RDS Snapshot/Point-in-time Recovery?

   A. The new DB instance created while restoring an RDS Snapshot or conducting an RDS point-in-time recovery will have a new endpoint.

   B. The new DB instance created while restoring an RDS Snapshot will have a new endpoint, but conducting an RDS point-in-time recovery will not.

C. The new DB instance created while conducting an RDS point-in-time recovery will have a new endpoint, but restoring an RDS Snapshot will not.

D. The new DB instance created while restoring an RDS Snapshot or conducting an RDS point-in-time recovery will not have a new endpoint.

19. Which of the following is a benefit of Amazon DynamoDB?

A. Ensures traffic distribution across all back-end instances irrespective of AZs.

B. Increases the need to keep equivalent number of back-end instances in each AZ.

C. Creates tables in high speed to scale to an unlimited number of items.

D. Supports large databases by allowing scaling up or down of clusters using magnetic disk storage or SSD.

20. Meg wants to increase storage and modify storage type on downtime, what should Meg know about increasing storage or modifying storage types?

A. Enhancing the allocated storage of an RDS instance doesn't result in outage/downtime, but changing the storage type to or from Magnetic Storage does.

B. Enhancing the allocated storage of an RDS instance doesn't result in out-

age/downtime, but changing the storage type to or from Provisioned IOPS Storage does.

C. Enhancing the allocated storage of an RDS instance results in outage/downtime, but changing the storage type to or from Magnetic Storage does not.

D. Enhancing the allocated storage of an RDS instance or modifying storage types both result in outage/downtime.

21. How does Amazon RDS handle Multi-AZ failover?

A. The IP address change is handled by AWS automatically and the customer doesn't have to manually change the connection string, in the case of a Multi-AZ failover.

B. The DNS change is handled by customer manually through the AWS CLI; the AWS cannot automatically change the connection string, in the case of a Multi-AZ failover.

C. The SSH change is handled by AWS automatically and the customer doesn't have to manually change the connection string, in the case of a Multi-AZ failover.

D. The DNS change is handled by AWS automatically and the customer doesn't have to manually change the connection string, in the case of a Multi-AZ failover.

22. Which of the following statements is true?

A. Currently Redshift supports Single-AZ and Multi-AZ deployments.

B. Currently Redshift only supports Single-AZ deployments, and not Multi-AZ.

C. Currently Redshift only supports Multi-AZ deployments, and not Single-AZ.

D. Currently Redshift supports only Multi-AZ deployments.

23. Which of the following describes how Redshift backs up data?

A. All data in a Redshift warehouse cluster is replicated at launch and also continuously and stored using ELB.

B. All data in a Redshift recordset cluster is copied at launch and also continuously and stored in Amazon S3.

C. All data in a Redshift warehouse cluster is replicated at launch and also continuously and stored in Amazon S3.

D. All data in a Redshift database cluster is distributed at launch and also continuously and stored in Amazon S3.

24. Jo wants to copy DynamoDB table across regions using AWS Data Pipeline, what should Jo know about copying DynamoDB data in regions using the AWS data pipeline?

A. DynamoDB Cross Regional Table Copy AWS Data Pipeline template configures periodic copying of data between DynamoDB tables within the same AWS regions only.

B. DynamoDB Cross Regional Table Copy AWS Data Pipeline template configures periodic copying of data between DynamoDB tables within or across AWS regions.

C. DynamoDB Cross Regional Table Copy AWS Data Pipeline template configures periodic copying of data between DynamoDB tables only across AWS regions.

D. DynamoDB Cross Regional Table Copy AWS Data Pipeline template configures archiving data between DynamoDB tables.

25. Ben wants to delete an RDS instance and wants to know whether Snapshots would be retained, what should Ben know about Snapshots of deleted RDS instances?

A. When an RDS instance is deleted, all manually created snapshots and the automatic snapshots are deleted along with the instance.

B. When an RDS instance is deleted, all manually created snapshots are retained and the automatic snapshots are deleted along with the instance.

C. When an RDS instance is deleted, all manually and automatically created snapshots are retained.

D. When an RDS instance is deleted, all automatically created snapshots are retained and the manual snapshots are deleted along with the instance.

26. What is the default maximum number of RDS instances per region?

  A. 5
  B. 40
  C. 50
  D. 100

27. Which of the following is a Database Engine that is supported by Amazon RDS?

  A. Firebird
  B. Amazon Aurora
  C. Microsoft Access
  D. Sybase

28. What is the default period of retention of RDS backups?

  A. 5 days
  B. 1 day
  C. 3 days
  D. 2 days

29. What is a Data Warehouse?

  A. Data Warehouse is a multidimensional analytical process which involves complex calculations, data modeling, and trend analysis.
  B. Data Warehouse is a central repository for data from one or many sources, used for complex querying, analysis, and report compilation via OLAP.
  C. Data Warehouse is a simple analysis of discovering patterns and trends with the use of sophisticated algorithms and is known as KDD.
  D. Data Warehouse is a process which looks at large data sets and tries to find correlations, patterns, and anomalies.

30. What would be the maximum size of a DynamoDB Item?

  A. 1024 bytes
  B. 200 KB
  C. 2048 bytes
  D. 400 KB

31. Which of the following describes how Redshift backs up data?

  A. Minimum of 3 copies of data is maintained: original, replica on compute nodes, and backup on S3.
  B. Snapshots can be synchronously replicated to S3 across regions.
  C. Minimum of 2 copies of data is maintained: original and replica on compute nodes.
  D. Snapshots can be asynchronously replicated across AWS regions.

32. Ed wants to know about effects of DB performance when backing up RDS Multi-AZ deployment, what should Ed know about RDS Multi-AZ deployment on DB performance?

  A. Although the backup is taken from the standby instance in Multi-AZ DB deployments, some latency can still occur for standby instances.
  B. No latency occurs when a backup is taken from the standby instance in Multi-AZ DB deployments.
  C. Although the backup is taken from the standby instance in Multi-AZ DB deployments, some latency can still occur for both master and standby instances.

D. Although the backup is taken from the standby instance in Multi-AZ DB deployments, some latency can still occur for master instances.

33. Pat wants to copy an RDS Snapshot across AWS regions, what should Pat know about copying RDS Snapshots?

A. Both automatic and manual snapshots of RDS instances can be copied from one AWS region to another.

B. Automatic and manual snapshots of RDS instances cannot be copied from one AWS region to another.

C. Manual snapshots of RDS instances can be copied from one AWS region to another, but automatic snapshots cannot be copied.

D. Automatic snapshots of RDS instances can be copied from one AWS region to another, but manual snapshots cannot be copied.

34. What is the default maximum number of read and write capacity units per DynamoDB table?

A. 10000 RCUs and 10000 WCUs

B. 10000 RCUs and 5000 WCUs

C. 5000 RCUs and 10000 WCUs

D. 5000 RCUs and 5000 WCUs

35. Which of the following is a type of workload for which Redshift would be better suited than RDS?

A. Workloads in which analytics can't interfere with OLAP

B. Workloads in which analytics can't interfere with OLTP

C. Pattern-matching and filtering workloads

D. Workloads with small data sets

36. Which of the following is an AWS service that supports data loading to Redshift?

A. ELB

B. MongoDB

C. S3

D. Remote SSL via standard output

37. What is the duration of RDS Multi-AZ Failover?

A. Two to three minutes.

B. One to three minutes.

C. One to two minutes.

D. Two to four minutes.

38. What is the maximum size of a result set returned by a DynamoDB query API call?

A. 1 TB

B. 2 MB

C. 1 MB

D. 1 GB

39. Which of the following is a benefit of RDS?

A. RDS ensures traffic distribution across all front-end instances with region-wise AZs.

B. RDS increases the need to keep equivalent number of back-end instances in each AZ.

C. RDS enhances an application's capacity to withstand the loss of one or more back-end instances.

D. RDS offers a consistent operational model for day-to-day administrative tasks.

40. Which of the following statements is true?

  A. RDS Provisioned IOPS Storage is not a single-tenant service and is shared by DB instances of other customers which can cause variations in performance.

  B. RDS Magnetic Storage is a single-tenant service and is shared by DB instances of other customers which can cause variations in performance.

  C. RDS Magnetic Storage is not a single-tenant service and cannot be shared by DB instances of other customers which can cause variations in performance.

  D. RDS Magnetic Storage is not a single-tenant service and is shared by DB instances of other customers which can

cause variations in performance.

41. Which of the following statements is true?

  A. AWS automatically fails over to a primary RDS instance in a different AWS region when the secondary becomes unavailable, by pointing the DB endpoint to a new IP address.

  B. AWS automatically fails over to a secondary RDS instance in a different AZ when the primary becomes unavailable, by pointing the DB endpoint to a new IP address.

  C. RDS CLI automatically fails over to a newly launched RDS instance in a different AZ when the primary becomes unavailable, by pointing the DB endpoint to a new IP address.

  D. AWS automatically fails over to a secondary RDS instance in the same AZ when the primary becomes unavailable, by updating the DB endpoint to an existing IP address.

# 8

# Events and Notifications

1. What is Receipt Handle in SQS?

   A. Receipt Handle is a unique identifier assigned by SQS to a message that it returns in the SendMessage response.

   B. Receipt Handle is an identifier assigned by SQS to a queue which is unique within all your queues, and needs to be given every time you want to perform any action on that queue.

   C. Receipt Handle is a message response component that is needed while deleting the message or changing the message visibility.

   D. Receipt Handle is a feature in SQS that allows you to provide structured metadata of messages which clients can use to better process messages.

2. What is an SWF Task List?

   A. SWF Task List is an SWF feature that offers a flexible way of routing tasks to workers, and to organize different tasks of a workflow.

   B. SWF Task List is an SWF feature that helps with interactions to other accounts without needing that account to assume IAM roles from your account.

   C. SWF Task List is an SWF feature that enables coordinating work across distributed components, giving you control over the implementation of tasks.

   D. SWF Task List is an SWF feature that runs activities in an AWS resource called a domain, and carries out a particular goal.

3. What is the characteristic of an SQS Access Control?

   A. SQS Access Control enables authentication of requests of any queues and messages and defines what operations can be performed.

   B. SQS Access Control enables assigning of policies to queues granting particular interactions to other accounts without needing that account to assume IAM roles from your account.

C. SQS Access Control enables assigning of policies to SQS components and defines the processing of messages by assuming IAM roles from your account.

D. SQS Access Control enables assigning of policies to SQS entities and defines their framework of operations.

4. Which of the following is a batch operation that is supported by Amazon SQS?

A. ReceiveMessageBatch

B. SendAllMessageBatch

C. ChangeVisibilityOfMessageBatch

D. DeleteAllMessageBatch

5. Which of the following is an option that can specify Message Attributes in SQS?

A. SQS Management Console

B. Receipt Handle API

C. AWS SDKs

D. AWS Devkit

6. Which of the following is a type of SNS client?

A. Publishers/service providers

B. Publishers/architects

C. Subscribers/service providers

D. Publishers/producers

7. What is Fanout in SNS?

A. Fanout in SNS is the process of subscribing multiple SQS queues to TLS endpoints with the help of AMS Management Console.

B. Fanout in SNS is the process of subscribing multiple SQS queues to a single SNS topic with the help SFTP.

C. Fanout in SNS is the process of replicating messages on SCP endpoints or email addresses.

D. Fanout in SNS is the process of subscribing multiple SQS queues to a single SNS topic with the help of AMS Management Console.

8. What is Visibility Timeout in SQS?

A. Visibility Timeout in SQS is the period of time in which SQS delays a message making it unavailable for other components from processing it.

B. Visibility Timeout in SQS is the period of time in which SQS makes a message invisible for other components from reprocessing it.

C. Visibility Timeout in SQS lets you postpone delivery of messages in a queue for a defined period of time, making messages invisible to consumers for that delay period.

D. Visibility Timeout in SQS is the period of time in which SQS makes a message unavailable for other components to receive/process as one component is already processing it.

9. What is the default maximum delay period for an SQS delay queue?

A. 10 minutes

B. 25 minutes

C. 15 minutes

D. 5 minutes

10. What is the characteristic of a Message Timer in SQS?

A. Message Timer is an SQS feature that lets you specify an initial period of time taken to receive a message you've added in a queue.

B. Message Timer is an SQS feature that lets you specify an initial period of time taken to process a message you've added in a queue.

C. Message Timer is an SQS feature that lets you specify an initial period of invisibility for a message you've added in a queue.

D. Message Timer is an SQS feature that lets you specify an initial period of time taken to send a message you've added in a queue.

11. What is the characteristic of an SQS Delay Queue?

A. SQS Delay Queue is a feature that lets you modify the delivery of messages in a queue for a defined period of time, making messages invisible to consumers for that delay period.

B. SQS Delay Queue is a feature that lets you postpone delivery of messages in a queue for a defined period of time, making messages invisible to consumers for that delay period.

C. SQS Delay Queue is a feature that lets you process messages in a queue for a defined period of time, making messages unavailable for reprocessing for that delay period.

D. SQS Delay Queue is a feature that lets you transfer messages in a queue for a defined period of time, making messages visible to consumers for that delay period.

12. Which of the following is a defined operation for Amazon SQS queue?

A. EraseQueue
B. DeleteAllMessageBatch
C. ChangeVisibilityOfMessageBatch
D. ListQueue

13. What is an SQS Unique ID?

A. SQS Unique Id is a globally unique message ID that SQS returns helps to change the message visibility.

B. SQS Unique Id is a globally unique message ID that SQS returns helps to set queue attributes and also to get URLs.

C. SQS Unique Id is a globally unique message ID that SQS returns when a message is delivered to the queue.

D. SQS Unique Id is a globally unique message ID that SQS returns helps to add and modify permissions.

14. Amy wants to know whether it is possible to receive a message from an SQS queue more than once, what does Amy need to know about message delivery in SQS?

A. SQS is designed for 'at least once' message delivery, so it is not possible that messages are delivered multiple times.

B. Although SQS is designed for 'at least once' message delivery, it is possible that messages are delivered multiple times.

C. SQS is designed for 'multiple times' message delivery, and messages are delivered multiple times.

D. SQS is designed for 'multiple times' message delivery and can also be delivered 'at least once'.

15. What is a Dead Letter Queue in SQS?

A. Dead Letter Queue is an AWS component that can be targeted by source queues to send messages which were not successfully processed.

B. Dead Letter Queue is an SQS supported queue that can be targeted by destination queues to change visibility of messages which were not successfully processed.

C. Dead Letter Queue is an SQS supported queue that can be targeted by source queues to send messages which were not successfully processed.

D. Dead Letter Queue is an SQS supported queue that can be targeted by destination queues to send messages which were successfully processed.

16. What is Queue URL in SQS?

A. Queue URL is an identifier assigned by SQS to a queue which is unique within all your queues, and needs to be given every time you want to perform any action on that queue.

B. Queue URL is a unique identifier assigned by SQS to a message that it returns in the SendMessage response.

C. Queue URL is a message response component that is needed while deleting the message or changing the message visibility.

D. Queue URL is a feature in SQS that allows you to provide structured metadata of messages which clients can use to better process messages.

17. Which of the following statements is true?

A. Access to SQS is granted or denied only based on the Security Groups, or a user created via AWS IAM.

B. Access to SQS is granted or denied only based on the account managers' approval, or a user created via AWS IAM.

C. Access to SQS is granted or denied only based on the account configurations, or a user created via AWS IAM.

D. Access to SQS is granted or denied only based on the AWS account, or a user created via AWS IAM.

18. What is the default maximum number of messages in an SQS queue?

A. Unlimited
B. 5000
C. Limited up to 100 GB
D. 4000

19. Which of the following can be described as a common use of Amazon SQS?

A. Amazon SQS provides highly latent and reliable storage for messages while they travel between servers.

B. Amazon SQS provides scalable and reliable storage for messages while they travel between servers.

C. Amazon SQS provides scalable and reliable storage for messages while they travel between AWS regions.

D. Amazon SQS provides scalable and reliable storage for record sets while they travel between AWS regions.

20. Which of the following statements is true?

A. Message IDs cannot be more than 200 characters in length.

B. Message IDs cannot be more than 256 characters in length.

C. Message IDs cannot be more than 128 characters in length.

D. Message IDs cannot be more than 100 characters in length.

21. How does Long Polling work?

A. How it works: Sends a WaitDateTimeSeconds argument to ReceiveMessage of upto 20 seconds.

B. How it works: Sends a WaitTimeSeconds argument to ReceiveMessage of upto 20 seconds.

C. How it works: Sends a WaitTimeSeconds argument to ReceiveMessage of upto 30 seconds.

D. How it works: Sends a WaitDateTimeSeconds argument to ReceiveMessage of upto 30 seconds.

22. Which of the following statements is true?

A. DeleteMessage: Delete a specific message.

B. DeleteMessageBatch: Delete all the messages in the queue without delete the queue.

C. DeleteMessage: Delete multiple messages which are marked for deletion.

D. PurgeQueue: Delete multiple messages.

23. Which of the following is a type of programmatic actor that SWF interacts with?

A. Workflow decider

B. Workflow starter

C. Activity starters

D. Workers

24. Which of the following is a component of a Message Attribute in SQS?

A. Name: containing character A-Z, a-z, 0-9, underscore, carat and backquote.

B. Data Type: String, Integer, Binary

C. Data Type: String, Number, Binary

D. Name: containing character A-Z, a-z, 0-9, underscore, hash and backquote.

25. Which of the following is an Amazon SWF component?

A. Workflow history

B. Units

C. Operations

D. Object Lists

26. What is a Message Attribute in SQS?

A. Message Attribute is a message response component that is needed while deleting the message or changing the message visibility.

B. Message Attribute is a unique identifier assigned by SQS to a message that it returns in the SendMessage response.

C. Message Attribute is an identifier assigned by SQS to a queue which is unique within all your queues, and needs to be given every time you want to perform any action on that queue.

D. Message Attribute is a feature in SQS that allows you to provide structured metadata of messages which clients can use to better process messages.

27. Which of the following statements is true?

A. How Long Polling works: The call will change the visibility of the message immediately if it appears before the time expires.

B. How Long Polling works: If there are messages in the queue, the call will process the message before returning upto WaitTimeSeconds.

C. How Long Polling works: The call will delay the message if it appears before the time expires.

D. How Long Polling works: If there is no message in the queue, the call will wait for a message before returning upto WaitTimeSeconds.

28. Which of the following statements is true?

A. The maximum size of an SQS message also includes timestamps and signatures.

B. The maximum size of an SQS message also includes geospatial data.

C. The maximum size of an SQS message does not include the message attributes (metadata).

D. The maximum size of an SQS message also includes the message attributes (metadata).

29. What is Long Polling in SQS?

A. Long Polling is a feature that helps to automatically batch multiple SendMessage to applications.

B. Long Polling is a feature that helps you determine if messages are available for inclusion in the response and is based on weighted random distribution.

C. Long Polling is a feature that helps you reduce cost and the load on your client by reducing empty responses to messages and ousting false empty responses.

D. Long Polling is a web service that uses multiple threads to process queues and increases the number of ReceiveMessageResponse instances returned.

# 9

## DNS

1. Which of the following is a DNS resource record type that is supported by Amazon Route 53?

   A. AAA
   B. IPC
   C. PCR
   D. A

2. Which of the following statements is true?

   A. Amazon Route 53 has enhanced networking capabilities with authoritative DNS service by ELB that stores user requests to infrastructure on AWS like EC3 instances and TLD balancers.
   B. Amazon Route 53 is a highly scalable and highly available authoritative DNS service by AWS that routes user requests to infrastructure on AWS like EC3 instances and ELB balancers.
   C. RDS is a highly scalable and highly available authoritative DNS service by AWS that routes user requests to infrastructure on AWS like EC3 instances and ELB balancers.

   D. Amazon Route 53 is a highly latent and highly scalable authoritative DNS service by AWS that authenticates user requests to infrastructure on AWS like EC3 instances and ELB balancers.

3. Which of the following statements is true?

   A. Responsive name server sends local data to the server to cache.
   B. Resolved data is sent to the server's browser to cache.
   C. Request for name server is sent to the user's browser to cache.
   D. Resolving name server sends this data to the user's browser to cache.

4. Which of the following is an Amazon Route 53 Weighted Routing Policy?

   A. Weighted Routing Policy: To route traffic depending on the end user's location.
   B. Weighted Routing Policy: To route a percentage of traffic to a specific resource.

C. Weighted Routing Policy: For routing traffic from resources in a primary location to a standby location.

D. Weighted Routing Policy: For when you have a single resource performing a given function for your domain.

5. Which of the following statements is true?

   A. * Applications can be protected from regional outage by being deployed in multiple AWS regions.

   B. * Applications can be protected from regional outage by being deployed across AZs with connection draining on.

   C. * Applications can be protected from regional outage by being spreading content world-wide with minimal client policy.

   D. * Applications can be protected from delegate request overloads by being deployed in multiple AWS regions.

6. What is a Route 53 Hosted Zone?

   A. A hosted zone is a compilation of resources record sets that are hosted by Amazon Route 53 and embedded anywhere on the front end of the user's website.

   B. A hosted zone is a compilation of resources that provides highly scalable and highly available DNS and is a reference to TCP or UDP.

   C. A hosted zone is a compilation of resource record sets hosted by Amazon Route 53

that are managed under a single domain name.

D. A hosted zone is a feature offered by Route 53 that allows you to have authoritative DNS records within a VPC without disclosing those records to the Internet.

7. Which of the following statements is true?

   A. Common routing policies: Simple Fail-rate Availability-based

   B. Common routing policies: Simple Weighted Latency-based

   C. Common routing policies: Simple Weighted-average Availability-based

   D. Common configuration policies: Simple Weighted Latency-based

8. Which of the following is a way in which an application can be built using Route 53 that is highly available and resilient?

   A. Health checks can make sure that applications delegate requests only to healthy EC2 instances.

   B. Latency-based routing policy can make sure that applications delegate requests only to healthy EC2 instances.

   C. ELB load balancers can make sure that applications delegate requests only to healthy EC2 instances.

   D. CloudFront edge can make sure that applications delegate requests only to healthy EC2 instances.

9. Which of the following is a step involved in DNS resolution?

A. Root server responds not with the answer, but with an address to a TLD server that has .com domain names information.

B. Resolving server asks one of the 23 root servers located across the world.

C. User's browser queries the TLD server for the IP address for amazon.com.

D. TLD server responds not with the answer, but with an address to a root server that has .com domain names information.

10. Which of the following is a record type in DNS?

A. PCR (Platform Configuration records)

B. CISO (Commercial Internet Security Option records)

C. SOA (Start of authority records)

D. IPC (Inter-process communication record)

11. What is IANA?

A. IANA is a body that controls a root zone database of all available TLDs.

B. IANA is a body that is responsible for evaluating SOCs.

C. IANA is a body that upgrades the physical security systems of the Key Management Facilities.

D. IANA is a body that ensures stable and unified global Internet.

12. What is Private DNS?

A. Private DNS is a feature offered by Route 53 allows you to configure split-view or split-horizon DNS through which you can maintain internal and external versions of the same application or website.

B. Private DNS is a feature offered by Route 53 allows you to configure full-view or full-horizon TLD through which you can maintain versions of the same application or website.

C. Private DNS is a feature offered by Route 53 that allows you to have authoritative DNS records within a VPC without disclosing those records to the Internet.

D. Private DNS is a feature offered by Route 53 that allows you to have TLD records within a VPC without re-routing those records to the Internet.

13. Which of the following is a step involved in DNS resolution?

A. Resolving server contacts the TLD server which provides the address for the RNS.

B. Resolving servers requests the DNS and receives authoritative records.

C. Resolving server contacts the DNS server which provides the address for the RNS.

D. Resolving servers requests the TLD and receives encrypted records.

14. Which of the following statements is true?

A. There are many record types in DNS. E.g.: A (Address mapping records) MS (Mail server records)

B. There are many record types in DNS. E.g.: A (Address mapping records) NS (Name server records)

C. There are many record types in DNS. E.g.: A (IP Version 6 address records) MS (Mapping exchanger record)

D. There are many record types in TLD. E.g.: A (Address mapping records) NS (Name server records)

15. What is an Alias?

A. Alias is a record type in the DNS zone that matches requests for the domain names on the basis of the configurations.

B. Alias is a service type in Route 53 that allows coordinating messages and enables applications or S3 website bucket to receive notifications.

C. Alias is a records type in Route 53 that holds data for the configuration of the DNS server or S3 website bucket or CloudFront distribution.

D. Alias is a records type in Route 53 that allows for the mapping of a zone apex DNS name to the account's ELB DNS name, or S3 website bucket or CloudFront distribution.

16. Which of the following is a step involved in DNS registration?

A. Domain names get individually registered in the cen-

tral database - the WhatIS database.

B. TLDs defining domain names are cached in a user's web browser.

C. Domain names get individually registered in the central database - the WhoIS database.

D. ELBs defining domain names are stored in a root zone database.

17. Nick wants to associate multiple IP addresses to a single record, how should Nick attempt this?

A. With Route 53, multiple IP addresses can be listed for an SOA record which configures web servers and S3 website buckets.

B. With Route 53, multiple IP addresses cannot be associated with a single record.

C. With Route 53, multiple IP addresses can be listed for an A record to balance the load of geographically balanced web servers.

D. With Route 53, multiple IP addresses can be listed for an AAAA record to balance the load of geographically balanced web servers.

18. Bill wants to create a CNAME record at a zone apex, how should Bill attempt this?

A. Route 53 doesn't allow you to create a CNAME record at a zone apex which is the top node of a DNS namespace.

B. Route 53 allows you to create a CNAME record at a zone apex to map the DNS name to the account's ELB DNS name.

C. Route 53 allows you to create a CNAME record at a zone apex on the basis of the configurations set up by you.

D. Route 53 allows you to create a CNAME record at a zone apex to balance the load of geographically balanced web servers.

19. Which of the following is a step involved in DNS registration?

A. Domains are registered with the hosted zone.

B. Domains are registered with domain registrars.

C. Domains are registered with the ELB zone.

D. Domains are registered with InterNIC where IANA maintains uniqueness of domain names all over the Internet.

20. What is the time taken for DNS changes to propagate globally?

A. Amazon Route 53 propagates the updates made to DNS records within 90 seconds to its world-wide network of authoritative DNS servers.

B. Amazon Route 53 propagates the updates made to DNS records within 120 seconds to its world-wide network of authoritative DNS servers.

C. Amazon Route 53 propagates the updates made to DNS records within 30 seconds to its world-wide network of authoritative DNS servers.

D. Amazon Route 53 propagates the updates made to DNS records within 60 seconds to its world-wide network of authoritative DNS servers.

21. Which of the following is an Amazon Route 53 Simple Routing Policy?

A. Simple Routing Policy: For routing traffic from resources in a primary location to a standby location.

B. Simple Routing Policy: To route a percentage of traffic to a specific resource.

C. Simple Routing Policy: For when you have a single resource performing a given function for your domain.

D. Simple Routing Policy: To route traffic depending on the end user's location.

22. What is a Wildcard Entry?

A. Wildcard Entry is a record in an ELB zone that will match requests for any domain name on the basis of the user requests.

B. Wildcard Entry is a record retrieved from the TLD server that will match requests on the queries raised by you.

C. Wildcard Entry is a record in a DNS zone that will match requests for any domain name on the basis of the configurations set up by you.

D. Wildcard Entry is a record retrieved from the DNS server which is mapped to the configurations set up by you.

# 10

# Caching

1. Which of the following statements is true?

   A. ElastiCache upgrades a Memcached Cluster manually if there is a need to protect against any network vulnerabilities.

   B. ElastiCache upgrades a Memcached Cluster manually if there is a need to protect against any patching vulnerabilities.

   C. ElastiCache upgrades a Redis Cluster automatically if there is a need to protect against any data vulnerabilities.

   D. ElastiCache upgrades a Memcached Cluster automatically if there is a need to protect against any security vulnerabilities.

2. What are the characteristics of Amazon ElastiCache?

   A. Amazon ElastiCache offers productive and reliable caching solutions for cloud applications, streamlining the launch and management of shared in-memory caching environment.

   B. Amazon ElastiCache offers cost-effective and scalable caching solutions for AWS applications, operating the distributed network of an in-memory caching environment.

   C. Amazon ElastiCache offers cost-effective and scalable caching solutions for cloud applications, streamlining the launch and management of distributed in-memory caching environment.

   D. Amazon ElastiCache offers cost-effective and highly latent caching solutions for cloud applications, streamlining the operations of an in-memory caching environment.

3. Which of the following statements is true?

   A. Benefits of In-Memory Caching: * Speeds up application's response time and enhances intractability with user interface.

B. Benefits of In-Memory Caching: * Speeds up messaging response time and enhances user experience.

C. Benefits of In-Memory Caching: * Speeds up notification response time and enhances user experience.

D. Benefits of In-Memory Caching: * Speeds up application's response time and enhances user experience.

4. What are the charges for ElastiCache Multi-AZ?

A. ElastiCache Multi-AZ feature is a node-based pay model, where the pay is computed on the nodes that you use.

B. ElastiCache Multi-AZ feature is available free of charge, you pay only for the nodes you use.

C. ElastiCache Multi-AZ feature is available on an hourly pay model, which includes charges for the nodes you use.

D. ElastiCache Multi-AZ feature is available on a monthly pay model, which includes charges for the nodes you use.

5. Which of the following is a benefit of In-Memory caching?

A. Cuts down the load on front-end data stores.

B. Cuts down the redundant data stores.

C. Helps you merge clusters quickly to store regularly used data.

D. Helps you launch clusters quickly to store regularly used data.

6. What is Elastic Load Balancing?

A. Elastic Load Balancing is a highly available AWS compute service that achieves failover whenever there is failure.

B. Elastic Load Balancing is a highly available AWS compute service that can manually be scaled to meet the requests of inbound traffic.

C. Elastic Load Balancing is a highly available AWS compute service that enables greater fault tolerance levels by distributing traffic across a group of EC2 instances in one or multiple AZs.

D. Elastic Load Balancing is a highly available AWS compute service that provides load balancing capacity by routing traffic to EC3 instances in same AWS regions.

7. What is a Relational Database?

A. Relational Database is the most commonly used database type that is organized like a tree structure with records connected to one another as links.

B. Relational Database is the most commonly used database type that offers a logical structure where the data can be stored, manipulated, and organized and looks like a graph.

C. Relational Database is the most commonly used database type that offers a common interface where users can read/write from the database through queries/commands written using SQL.

D. Relational Database is the most commonly used database type which is like an upside-down tree structure with multiple member records or files linked to multiple owner files.

8. What is the structure of an ElastiCache Redis Replication Group?

A. An ElastiCache cluster for the root node with children nodes as replicas, and each of those clusters with a single node.

B. An ElastiCache cluster for the master node with extra clusters as replicas, and each of those clusters with multiple nodes.

C. An ElastiCache cluster for the parent node with extra clusters as replicas, and each of the instance types with a single node.

D. An ElastiCache cluster for the master node with extra clusters as replicas, and each of those clusters with a single node.

9. What are Prime Candidates for Caching?

A. Often, data elements accessed with page activation or with every request, but remain consistent are the prime candidates for caching.

B. Often, data elements accessed on every page load or with every request, but remain unchanged are the prime candidates for caching.

C. Data elements that are accessed on every event load or when you make requests but do not change are usually the prime candidates for caching.

D. Data elements that are accessed on every page load or when the account owners make requests and remain unmodified are usually the prime candidates for caching.

10. What is a Maintenance Window?

A. Maintenance Window is the 60 minute time duration specified during configuration when either requested or required software updates occur in Amazon ElastiCache.

B. Maintenance Window is the 120 minute time duration specified by the customer when either requested or required software patching occurs in Amazon ElastiCache.

C. Maintenance Window is the 60 minute time duration specified by the customer when either requested or required software patching occurs in Amazon ElastiCache.

D. Maintenance Window is the 60 minute time duration specified by the account owner when either requested or required data backups are taken in Amazon Elasti-Cache.

11. What is the characteristic of an SQS Delay Queue?

    A. SQS Delay Queue is a feature that lets you modify the delivery of messages in a queue for a defined period of time, making messages invisible to consumers for that delay period.

    B. SQS Delay Queue is a feature that lets you postpone delivery of messages in a queue for a defined period of time, making messages invisible to consumers for that delay period.

    C. SQS Delay Queue is a feature that lets you process messages in a queue for a defined period of time, making messages unavailable for reprocessing for that delay period.

    D. SQS Delay Queue is a feature that lets you transfer messages in a queue for a defined period of time, making messages visible to consumers for that delay period.

12. Which of the following is a scaling mechanism for Memcached ElastiCache cluster?

    A. Limit the replication group.
    B. Add instance types to the cluster.
    C. Create a new cluster with a smaller instance type.
    D. Add nodes to the cluster.

13. How many read replicas can be created per ElastiCache Master Cluster?

    A. You can create upto 10 read replicas for any primary cache node in ElastiCache.

    B. You can create upto 5 read replicas for any primary cache node in ElastiCache.

    C. You can create upto 15 read replicas for any primary cache node in ElastiCache.

    D. You can create upto 6 read replicas for any primary cache node in ElastiCache.

14. What is a use case for Redis?

    A. Redis can be used for Data backup and restore options.

    B. Redis can be used if you require advanced functions like scoreboards, or filter and rank.

    C. Redis can be used if you require a simple, easily partitionable, and horizontally latent in-memory component store.

    D. Redis can be used if you require a simple, easily partitionable, and horizontally scalable in-memory object store.

15. Which of the following is a benefit of caching for databases?

    A. Offloading caching requests to the cache tier will alleviate pressure.

    B. Cache-aside pattern helps filter results before checking the cache tier.

    C. Offloading read requests to the cache tier will alleviate pressure.

    D. Cache-aide pattern helps check cache tier before checking the database.

16. Which of the following describes how Memcached Auto Discovery works?

    A. ElastiCache cluster adds a node to an endpoint.

    B. The cluster endpoint (TLS record) holds TLS names of all the nodes belonging to the cluster.

    C. ElastiCache cluster gets a unique configuration endpoint.

    D. The configuration endpoint (CNAME record) holds CNAMES of all the nodes belonging to the instance type.

17. Which of the following statements is true?

    A. If a software patching is included in the maintenance, ElastiCache Nodes would not face downtime during the maintenance window.

    B. If a data backup is included in the maintenance, Elasti-Cache Nodes might not face downtime during the maintenance window.

    C. If a software patching is included in the maintenance, ElastiCache Nodes might face downtime during the maintenance window.

    D. If a restore option is included in the maintenance, ElastiCache Nodes might not face downtime during the maintenance window.

18. Which of the following statements is true?

    A. Memcached ElastiCache cluster type can be expanded vertically by choosing a smaller or larger node type that matches your needs, but Redis cluster types cannot be expanded.

    B. Redis ElastiCache cluster type can be expanded vertically by choosing a smaller or larger node type that matches your needs, but Memcached cluster types cannot be expanded.

    C. Both ElastiCache cluster types, Memcached and Redis, cannot be expanded vertically.

    D. Both ElastiCache cluster types, Memcached and Redis, can be expanded vertically by choosing a smaller or larger node type that matches your needs.

19. How can Prime Candidates for Caching be identified?

    A. Prime candidate elements can be identified by analyzing security groups, regularly run queries, and provisioned nodes.

    B. Prime candidate elements can be identified by analyzing defined clusters of data, regularly run queries, and expensive operations.

    C. Prime candidate elements can be identified by analyzing patterns of data usage, regularly run queries, and expensive operations.

    D. Prime candidate elements can be identified by analyzing patterns of data usage, regular API calls, and expensive operations.

20. Tom wants to access an Elasti-Cache node from the public in-

ternet, how should Tom access an ElastiCache node?

A. You cannot access an ElastiCache node from the public internet, you must be within the EC2 network, and authorized through relevant security groups.

B. You cannot access an ElastiCache node from the public internet; you must be within the EC3 network to access the nodes.

C. You can easily access an ElastiCache node from the public internet.

D. You cannot access an ElastiCache node from the public internet, you must be within the AWS regions, and authorized by account owners.

21. Meg wants to change an Elas-tiCache cluster's instance type, what should Meg know about changing node instance types of ElastiCache clusters?

A. You can dynamically change an ElastiCache cluster's node instance type by specifying limits for the cluster.

B. You can dynamically change an ElastiCache cluster's node instance type.

C. You cannot dynamically change an ElastiCache cluster's node instance type, but you can override the default configuration as you specify limits for the cluster.

D. You cannot dynamically change an ElastiCache cluster's node instance type, but you can create a new cluster when you scale up or down.

# 11

# Additional Services

1. What is the maximum size of a Kinesis record's data blob?

   A. The maximum size of a Kinesis record's data blob is 1 TB.

   B. The maximum size of a Kinesis record's data blob is 3 MB.

   C. The maximum size of a Kinesis record's data blob is 2 MB.

   D. The maximum size of a Kinesis record's data blob is 1 MB.

2. Which of the following describes what Amazon CloudFront is suitable for?

   A. Amazon CloudFront is suitable for: Popular dynamic and static content where users are not geographically dispersed.

   B. Amazon CloudFront is suitable for: Popular dynamic and static content where users are distributed geographically.

   C. Amazon CloudFront is suitable for: Resources where all users are at the same location or are connecting via a corporate VPN.

   D. Amazon CloudFront is suitable for: Building custom applications for real time processing and analysis of streaming data

3. Which of the following can be considered as information recorded by CloudTrail?

   A. Time of the request

   B. Call parameters

   C. Name of the API

   D. Identity of the service

4. What is the ideal mix for Clusters used in app testing?

   A. Clusters used in app testing: Master: on-demand; Core: on-demand; Task: on-demand

   B. Clusters used in app testing: Master: on-demand; Core: on-demand; Task: spot

   C. Clusters used in app testing: Master: on-demand; Core: spot; Task: spot

D. Clusters used in app testing: Master: spot; Core: spot; Task: spot

5. Which of the following is a CloudFront Origin Setting?

   A. Origin URL

   B. Origin Access Identity (Glacier only)

   C. Origin Key ID

   D. Origin Domain Name

6. Which of the following is an AWS Storage and Content Delivery Service?

   A. AWS CloudTrail

   B. AWS Key Management Service (KMS)

   C. AWS CloudHSM

   D. Amazon CloudFront

7. Which of the following is a Geo Restriction option in Cloud-Front?

   A. Using CloudFront Geo Restriction feature: restricts access to all files associated with a distribution, at a country level.

   B. Using 3rd Geolocation services: restricts access to all files in distribution, at country level than at a granular level.

   C. Using 3rd Geolocation services: restricts access to users at a country level.

   D. Using CloudFront Geo Restriction feature: restricts access to files associated with a defined size, at a country level.

8. What is the maximum amount of data that can be stored in Gateway-Cached appliances?

A. Gateway-Cached volume: 384 TB (12 volumes, each 32 TB in size)

B. Gateway-Cached volume: 512 TB (32 volumes, each 16 TB in size)

C. Gateway-Cached volume: 1 PB (32 volumes, each 32 TB in size)

D. Gateway-Cached volume: 192 TB (12 volumes, each 16 TB in size)

9. Christian wants to reserve CloudFront capacity, what are the reserved capacity pricing options that Christian should be aware of?

   A. CloudFront offers reserved capacity pricing in which you get a considerable discount by committing to a minimum monthly usage level for 15 months or more.

   B. CloudFront offers reserved capacity pricing in which you get a limited discount by committing to a maximum monthly usage level for 12 months or more.

   C. CloudFront offers reserved capacity pricing in which you get a considerable discount by committing to a minimum monthly usage level for 12 months or more.

   D. CloudFront offers reserved capacity pricing in which you get a limited discount by committing to a maximum monthly usage level for 24 months or more.

10. Which of the following is a functionality that can be configured in a CloudFront Cache Behavior?

A. Functionalities that can be configured in a CloudFront Cache Behavior: Whether to require Dedicated IP custom SSL or not.

B. Functionalities that can be configured in a CloudFront Cache Behavior: Whether to require SSL or not.

C. Functionalities that can be configured in a CloudFront Cache Behavior: Whether to forward query strings to the servers or not.

D. Functionalities that can be configured in a CloudFront Cache Behavior: Origin for forwarding requests (for multi-origin distributions).

11. Which of the following is an OpsWorks Lifecycle event?

A. Initialize

B. Deactivate

C. Setup

D. Activate

12. What is the maximum capacity of a Storage Gateway VTL?

A. You can store upto 1200 virtual tapes in a Storage Gateway VTL, not exceeding the maximum size limit of 120 TB.

B. You can store upto 1500 virtual tapes in a Storage Gateway VTL, not exceeding the maximum size limit of 150 TB.

C. You can store upto 1400 virtual tapes in a Storage Gateway VTL, not exceeding the maximum size limit of 140 TB.

D. You can store upto 1600 virtual tapes in a Storage Gateway VTL, not exceeding the maximum size limit of 160 TB.

13. What is the maximum size of Gateway-Stored volume?

A. 1 PB

B. 16 TB

C. 192 TB

D. 32 TB

14. Which of the following describes a Use Case of CloudFront Signed Cookie?

A. CloudFront Signed Cookies - Use Cases: If you do not want your current URLs changed.

B. CloudFront Signed Cookies - Use Cases: If you choose to use an R™P distribution.

C. CloudFront Signed Cookies - Use Cases: If you want access restriction on individuals.

D. CloudFront Signed Cookies - Use Cases: If your users are using clients that do not support cookies.

15. What is AWS Storage Gateway?

A. AWS Storage Gateway is a service that offers a scalable, fully managed storage service that offers a simple, cost-effective way to decouple the components of a cloud infrastructure.

B. AWS Storage Gateway is a service that connects on-premises applications offering scalable storage solutions for cloud applications and management of distributed in-memory caching environment.

C. AWS Storage Gateway is a service that streamlines the setup, operations, and scaling of database on AWS, making it easy for customers to focus on application and schema.

D. AWS Storage Gateway is a service that connects your IT environment with AWS storage infrastructure, maintains regularly accessed data on-premises, and encrypts and stores all data on S3 or Glacier.

16. Which of the following is an origin supported by Amazon CloudFront?

A. Amazon S3 Origin Access Identifiers

B. AWS WAF Web ACL

C. AWS Directory Service for Microsoft Active Directory (Enterprise Edition)

D. Amazon S3 websites

17. Which of the following statements is true?

A. Storage Gateway Cached and Storage Gateway Virtual Tape Shelves are stored on Amazon S3.

B. Storage Gateway Cached and Storage Gateway Virtual Tape Shelves are stored on Amazon Glacier.

C. Storage Gateway Virtual Tape Libraries are stored on Amazon S3, and Storage Gateway Virtual Tape Shelves are stored on Amazon Glacier.

D. Storage Gateway Virtual Tape Libraries are stored on Amazon Glacier, and Storage Gateway Virtual Tape Shelves are stored on Amazon S3.

18. Which of the following is a component of AWS Elastic Beanstalk?

A. Application configurations

B. Environment

C. Environment versions

D. Application templates

19. Which of the following is a configuration of AWS Storage Gateway?

A. Gateway-VPC

B. Gateway-EMR

C. Gateway-Cached

D. Gateway-R$^{TM}$P

20. What is AWS CloudTrail?

A. AWS CloudTrail is a service that uses dedicated API appliances in AWS cloud to help organizations meet regulatory, contractual, and corporate data security compliance requirements.

B. AWS CloudTrail is a service that controls generation of cryptographic keys and the operations offered by HSM and help to store sensitive data.

C. AWS CloudTrail is a service that uses VPC and improves the network performance in multiple regions.

D. AWS CloudTrail is a security service that makes user activity visible by recording API calls made on your account, helping you track changes made to your resources.

21. Chris wants to use CloudFront to serve dynamic content, what should Chris know of dynamic content on CloudFront?

    A. You cannot use CloudFront to serve dynamic content, irrespective of the content type.

    B. You can now use CloudFront to serve dynamic content, making applications faster and more responsive, irrespective of where your users are situated.

    C. You can now use Cloud-Front to serve dynamic content, but is limited to the content type of the subset of files which are in distribution.

    D. You cannot use CloudFront to serve dynamic content, irrespective of the subset of files in distribution.

22. Which of the following is an Import source supported by AWS Import/Export?

    A. Amazon VPC

    B. AWS Snowball

    C. AWS ELB

    D. Amazon S3

23. Which of the following is a scaling option for OpsWorks instances?

    A. Capacity-base

    B. Automatic Scaling (24/7)

    C. Time-based

    D. Memory-based

24. Which of the following statements is true?

    A. You can integrate CloudHSM with Amazon RDS only for DB2 instances, allowing AWS to operate DB2 databases while you still control master encryption keys.

    B. You can integrate CloudHSM with Amazon RDS only for Oracle instances, allowing AWS to operate Oracle databases while you still control master encryption keys.

    C. You can integrate CloudHSM with Redshift only for Oracle instances, allowing AWS to operate Oracle databases while you still control master encryption keys.

    D. You can integrate CloudHSM with Amazon VPC only for EC2 instances, allowing AWS to operate EC2 databases while you still control master encryption keys.

25. Which of the following is a type of AWS Import/Export?

    A. AWS Backup/Retrieval Services

    B. AWS Import/Export Services

    C. AWS On-Demand Disk

    D. AWS Snowball

26. Which of the following is a Use Case for Amazon Kinesis Firehose?

    A. Firehose: Analyzing streaming data real time using standard SQL.

B. Firehose: Building custom applications for real time processing and analysis of streaming data.

C. Firehose: Loading huge volumes of streaming traffic into AWS.

D. Firehose: Loading huge volumes of streaming data into AWS.

27. Chris wants to use a Storage Gateway snapshot to create an EBS volume, what should Chris know about using Storage Gateway snapshot to create EBS volume?

A. Amazon allows you to take point-in-time snapshots of Gateway-Cached volume data in Amazon S3 in the form of Amazon EBS snapshots.

B. Amazon allows you to take point-intercept snapshots of Gateway-Stored volume data in Amazon VPC in the form of Amazon EBS snapshots.

C. Amazon allows you to take point-intercept snapshots of Gateway-VTL volume data in RDS in the form of Amazon EBS snapshots.

D. Amazon allows you to take static snapshots of Gateway-VTL volume data in Amazon S3 in the form of Amazon EBS snapshots.

28. Which of the following is a type of Amazon Kinesis Service?

A. Amazon Kinesis Analysis

B. Amazon Kinesis Strings

C. Amazon Kinesis Firehose

D. Amazon Kinesis Firestreams

29. Which of the following is a language supported by Elastic Beanstalk?

A. REXX

B. Node.js

C. JSON

D. Julia

30. Which of the following is an option for CloudFront to deliver HTTPS content in the client's domain name?

A. Dedicated IP custom SCP

B. CDP custom SSL

C. RDP custom TLS

D. Dedicated IP custom SSL

31. Which of the following describes a method with which CloudFront can serve private content?

A. OpsWorks Stack

B. Signed URLs

C. Unsigned cookies

D. Unsigned URLs

32. Which of the following is a step describing how Amazon CloudFront works?

A. Amazon CloudFront first initiates data to be copied on to a physical storage appliance at the source.

B. Amazon CloudFront first uses geolocation to identify geographic locations of users and optimize downloads.

C. Amazon CloudFront first initiates appliances to be shipped via traditional shipping methods.

D. Amazon CloudFront first initiates data to be copied on to the destination.

33. Which of the following is a benefit of CloudFront?

   A. Low latency
   B. High Scalability
   C. High Storability
   D. High Availability

34. Which of the following describes when to use AWS Directory Service for Microsoft Active Directory?

   A. When you need to set up a dynamic relationship between on-premises directories and an AWS central directory.
   B. When there are more than 15000 users.
   C. When there are more than 5000 users.
   D. When you need to set up a trust relationship between off-premises directories and an AWS central directory.

35. Which of the following can be described as a part of the Cloud-Front Distribution Details?

   A. Default Root Object
   B. S3 bucket access
   C. Alternate domain names (CNAMEs)
   D. HTTP/HTTPS ports

36. What is the Use Case of a Gateway-Cached volume?

   A. Gateway-Cached: Expands on-premises storage to S3, and caches frequently used files locally.
   B. Gateway-Cached: Keeps all data available locally at all times, and replicates all data to S3 asynchronously.

   C. Gateway-Cached: Keeps backup tape software and processes, and stores data in the cloud to get rid of physical tapes.
   D. Gateway-Cached: Keeps all data backups locally at all times, and retrieves all data synchronously.

37. What is the ideal mix for Long-running EMR Clusters?

   A. Long-running EMR clusters: Master: spot; Core: spot; Task: spot
   B. Long-running EMR clusters: Master: on-demand; Core: on-demand; Task: spot
   C. Long-running EMR clusters: Master: on-demand; Core: on-demand; Task: on-demand
   D. Long-running EMR clusters: Master: on-demand; Core: spot; Task: spot

38. Which of the following statements is true?

   A. Tapes ejected by backup software from a VTL are moved to a VTS located in Glacier, for long-term storage/archiving purposes.
   B. Tapes ejected by backup software from a VTL are moved to a VTS located in S3, for short-term storage/archiving purposes.
   C. Tapes ejected by backup software from a VTL are moved to a VTS located in Glacier, for short-term storage/archiving purposes.
   D. Tapes ejected by backup software from a VTL are moved

to a VTS located in S3, for long-term storage/archiving purposes.

39. What is Key Management?

   A. Key Management is the management of symmetric keys in a cryptosystem which includes their definition, attestation, and exchange.

   B. Key Management is the management of asymmetric keys in a cryptosystem which includes their creation, exchange, use, storage, and replacement.

   C. Key Management is the management of cryptographic keys in a cryptosystem which includes their definition, attestation, and exchange.

   D. Key Management is the management of cryptographic keys in a cryptosystem which includes their creation, exchange, use, storage, and replacement.

40. Which of the following is an AWS OpsWorks Component that can be defined by the customer?

   A. Package configuration

   B. Software installation

   C. Architecture of an application

   D. Architecture of resources

41. Mike wants to upload content through CloudFront, how should Mike attempt this?

   A. You cannot upload content to your web servers through CloudFront using the existing distributions for upload requests.

   B. You can now upload content to your web servers through CloudFront using the existing distributions for upload requests by connecting through VPN.

   C. You can now upload content to your web servers through CloudFront using the existing distributions for upload requests by using AWS CLI.

   D. You can now upload content to your web servers through CloudFront using the existing distributions for upload requests by turning on support in the AWS MC.

42. What is Geo restriction in Cloud-Front?

   A. Geo restriction in Cloud-Front is a feature through which you can block content from specific locations from being uploaded through your CloudFront web distribution.

   B. Geo restriction in Cloud-Front is a feature through which you can administer content from specific locations from being modified through your Cloud-Front web distribution.

   C. Geo restriction in Cloud-Front is a feature through which you can block users in specific locations from accessing content being distributed through your CloudFront web distribution.

   D. Geo restriction in Cloud-Front is a feature through which you can filter users in specific locations from limited access to content distributed through your CloudFront web distribution.

43. Which of the following is an available Elastic Beanstalk environment tier?

   A. Environment Tier
   B. Worker Types
   C. Web Server Services
   D. Web Server Tier

44. What is an AWS Directory Service?

   A. AWS Directory Service is a managed service that synchronizes data to the AWS Cloud through various administration tools.

   B. AWS Directory Service is a managed service that provides directories containing information about a client organization like the users, computers, groups, and other resources.

   C. AWS Directory Service is a managed service that provides administration tools to manage signed URLs, signed cookies, and other resources.

   D. AWS Directory Service is a managed service that provides features for fine-grained control to backup and archive data.

# 12

# Security

1. What is the type of Cryptography that is used in Amazon EC2?

   A. EC2 uses private-key cryptography, which means a private key is used to encrypt data and also used by the recipient to decrypt data.

   B. EC2 uses secret-key cryptography, which means a private key is used to encrypt data, and a secret key is used by the recipient to decrypt data.

   C. EC2 uses secret-key cryptography, which means a secret key is used to encrypt data, and a public key is used by the recipient to decrypt data.

   D. EC2 uses public-key cryptography, which means a public key is used to encrypt data, and a private key is used by the recipient to decrypt data.

2. Which of the following is a characteristic of a Security Group Rule?

   A. Applied at the subnet level

   B. Rules cannot be aggregated to create one single set

   C. Deny by default

   D. Stateless

3. How can High-Availability Design within AWS be achieved?

   A. High-Availability Design within AWS can be achieved through boundary devices like firewalls that monitor and control information flow at internal/external boundaries using rule sets, configurations, and ACLs.

   B. High-Availability Design within AWS can be achieved through boundary devices like firewalls that monitor and control information flow and helps to build a reliable base in case of any failover.

   C. High-Availability Design within AWS can be achieved by merging applications from various Availability Zones which helps build centralized control over system failure modes.

D. High-Availability Design within AWS can be achieved by distributing applications across various Availability Zones which helps build resilience towards a lot of system failure modes.

4. Which of the following statements is true?

A. Securing Connections: Connections between your DB Instance and your application can be encrypted using mathematical algorithms.

B. Securing Connections: Connections between your DB Instance and your EC2 instances can be encrypted using SSL.

C. Securing Connections: Connections between your DB Instance and your application can be encrypted using SSH keys.

D. Securing Connections: Connections between your DB Instance and your application can be encrypted using SSL.

5. What is AWS CloudTrail?

A. Amazon CloudTrail is a managed service that allows you to generate and control encryption keys which can be used to encrypt and decrypt your data as per the policies you specify.

B. AWS CloudTrail is a security service that makes user activity visible by recording API calls made on your account, helping you track changes made to your resources.

C. Amazon CloudTrail is a global CDN service that combines with other AWS products to offer businesses and developers an easy way of content distribution to end users.

D. Amazon CloudTrail is a service that uses dedicated HSM appliances in AWS cloud to help organizations meet regulatory, contractual, and corporate data security compliance requirements.

6. Which of the following best describes what rotation of keys can secure?

A. IAM User Accounts

B. AWS Resources

C. IAM Devices

D. AWS Actions

7. Which of the following describes a step to access the WorkSpaces?

A. WorkSpaces grants access to users only after they successfully sign in with either the software tokens, or a set of unique user credentials.

B. WorkSpaces grants access to users only after they successfully sign in with either their Active Directory credentials, or a set of unique credentials.

C. WorkSpaces grants access to object owners only after they successfully sign in with either their AWS credentials, or a set of unique credentials.

D. WorkSpaces grants access to users only after they successfully sign in with either their new Cognito credentials, or a set of unique credentials.

8. Which of the following statements is true?

   A. Access Control: Access to AWS components can be controlled via DB security groups.

   B. Access Control: Access to Instances can be controlled via SSL.

   C. Access Control: Access to AWS components can be controlled using SSL.

   D. Access Control: Access to Instances can be controlled via DB security groups.

9. Which of the following statements is true?

   A. AWS allows EC2 instances running in promiscuous mode to sniff traffic by using their own MAC/source IP addresses.

   B. AWS allows EC2 instances running in promiscuous mode to sniff traffic that is targeted for some other virtual instance.

   C. AWS does not allow EC2 instances running in promiscuous mode to sniff traffic that is targeted for some other virtual instance.

   D. AWS does not allow EC2 instances running in promiscuous mode to sniff traffic by using their own DMAC address.

10. What is Loose Coupling?

   A. Loose Coupling is the practice of coupling system components so that they depend on each other directly.

   B. Loose Coupling is the practice of coupling system components as loosely as possible to reduce interdependencies, which in turn prevents failure of other components when one fails.

   C. Loose Coupling is the practice of coupling system components which are highly dependent on each other and components assume multiple responsibilities.

   D. Loose Coupling is the practice of coupling AWS services and refers to the approach of interconnecting services.

11. Which of the following statements is true?

   A. Security Standards and Certifications AWS is in compliance with: * PSA * DIACAP * ISO 9001, ISO 22000, and ISO 27001

   B. Security Standards and Certifications AWS is in compliance with: * IANA * DIACAP * ISO 9002, ISO 27001, and ISO 27018

   C. Security Standards and Certifications AWS is in compliance with: * FISMA * GSA * ISO 9002, ISO 22000, and ISO 27018

   D. Security Standards and Certifications AWS is in compliance with: * FISMA * DIACAP * ISO 9001, ISO 27001, and ISO 27018

12. Which of the following statements is true?

   A. You can associate one or more security groups to one

or more of your EC2 instances at the time of launching the instances, and also add/modify rules later.

B. You can associate one or more security groups to one or more of your EC2 instances at the time of launching the instances, adding and modifying rules later is not possible as they are immutable.

C. You can associate one security group to only one of your EC2 instances at the time of launching the instances, and you cannot modify rules later.

D. You can associate one security group to only one of your EC2 instances at the time of launching the instances, and also add/modify rules later.

13. Which of the following statements is true?

A. Network traffic in EC2 instances can be spoofed as AWS permits instances to send traffic using MAC/source IP addresses.

B. Network traffic in EC2 instances cannot be spoofed as AWS permits instances to send traffic using only their own MAC/source IP addresses.

C. Network traffic in EC2 instances cannot be spoofed as AWS permits instances to send traffic using only their own DMAC address and testing the ARP reply.

D. Network traffic in EC2 instances can be spoofed as AWS permits instances to send traffic using DMAC address.

14. Which of the following statements is true?

A. To grant initial access to an instance, EC2 supports RSA 2056 SSH-2 Key pairs.

B. To grant initial access to an instance, EC2 supports AES 192 SSH-2 Key pairs.

C. To grant initial access to an instance, EC2 supports RSA 2048 SSH-2 Key pairs.

D. To grant initial access to an instance, EC2 supports AES 128 SSH-2 Key pairs.

15. Which of the following is an AWS service that supports encryption of data at rest?

A. ELB

B. CloudTrail

C. DynamoDB

D. Amazon S3

16. Mark wants to connect to EC2 Instances on Linux using key pairs, how should Mark attempt this?

A. As Linux instances don't have passwords, you login using the SSH private key.

B. Login with assigned passwords to connect EC2 instances on Linux.

C. As Linux instances don't have passwords, you login using AES keys.

D. As Linux instances don't have passwords, you first obtain the administrator password using the private key, and then sign in with RDP.

17. Which of the following is a Security and Identity service offered by AWS?

    A. AWS IAM
    B. AWS CloudTrail
    C. AWS Lambda
    D. AWS Config

18. Which of the following is an authentic protocol supported by Amazon WorkSpaces?

    A. Kerberos
    B. TACACS
    C. RADIUS
    D. DIAMETER

19. Which of the following statements is true?

    A. Access to SQS is granted or denied only based on the Security Groups, or a user created via AWS IAM.
    B. Access to SQS is granted or denied only based on the account managers' approval, or a user created via AWS IAM.
    C. Access to SQS is granted or denied only based on the account configurations, or a user created via AWS IAM.
    D. Access to SQS is granted or denied only based on the AWS account, or a user created via AWS IAM.

20. Which of the following is a security feature within Amazon VPC?

    A. Security groups
    B. Routing Gateways
    C. External Tables
    D. DACL

21. Which of the following is a key in Amazon Redshift Encryption Architecture?

    A. Recordset Key
    B. Transaction Key
    C. Dataset Key
    D. Data encryption keys

22. How can controlling network access to ElastiCache Cache Clusters be achieved?

    A. You can control network access to your ElastiCache Cache Clusters through SQS via AWS IAM.
    B. You can control network access to your ElastiCache Cache Clusters through Cache Security Groups which via RADIUS server.
    C. You can control network access to your ElastiCache Cache Clusters through Cache Security Groups which play the role of a firewall.
    D. You can control network access to your ElastiCache Cache Clusters through Amazon Cognito which offer identify services.

23. Which of the following is a type of credential used by AWS for authentication?

    A. MFA
    B. SFA
    C. Signed Cookies
    D. Signed URLs

24. Which of the following can be described as a security feature on Amazon S3?

    A. Access on S3 is restricted by default, letting only owners of S3 buckets the rights.

B. Uploads and downloads are secured through SSH key pairs.

C. Access on S3 is unrestricted by default, and you can later configure the rights of owners of S3 buckets.

D. Many other encryption options are available to protect data in motion.

25. Which of the following is a step for Amazon Cognito to provide identity and sync services for mobile and web-based applications?

A. Amazon Cognito returns the function call and new permanent AWS credentials with restricted privileges, to the user.

B. Amazon Cognito returns a new token, and new permanent AWS credentials with unrestricted privileges, to the user.

C. Amazon Cognito returns a new ID, and new permanent AWS tokens with unrestricted privileges, to the user.

D. Amazon Cognito returns a new ID, and new temporary AWS credentials with restricted privileges, to the user.

26. What are API endpoints in AWS?

A. API endpoints in AWS are customer access points placed by AWS that allow secure sessions via HTTPS access, enabling you to monitor inbound/outbound network traffic more comprehensively.

B. API endpoints in AWS are unique URLs that represent objects or group of objects, and enable monitoring of various AWS components more comprehensively.

C. API endpoints in AWS are customer access points placed by AWS making it easy to build HTTP services and RESTful applications, and reach clients more comprehensively.

D. API endpoints in AWS refer to objects or a group of objects that are exposed to a URL which can accept web requests that may or may not be RESTful.

27. What is a Key Pair?

A. Private and secret keys together are called a key pair, which you create while logging in to your instance the first time, and specify at the time of each launch.

B. Private keys and biometrics together are called a key pair, which you create while logging in to your instance the first time, and specify at the time of each launch.

C. Private and public keys together are called a key pair, which you create while logging in to your instance the first time, and specify at the time of each launch.

D. Public and secret keys together are called a key pair, which you create while logging in to your instance the first time, and specify at the time of each launch.

28. Which of the following is a step for Amazon Cognito to provide identity and sync services for mobile and web-based applications?

A. Client application authenticates with an account owner using their SDK.

B. Client application authenticates with an account owner using the AWS CLI.

C. Client application authenticates with an identity provider (e.g. Google) using the AWS CLI.

D. Client application authenticates with an identity provider (e.g. Google) using their SDK.

29. What is the Shared Responsibility Model?

A. Shared Responsibility model is a security model used by AWS where AWS ensures availability of the cloud infrastructure, and requires customers to scale workloads deployed in their AWS accounts.

B. Shared Responsibility model is a security model used by AWS where AWS ensures security of the cloud infrastructure, and requires customers to secure workloads deployed in their AWS accounts.

C. Shared Responsibility model is a security model which includes global infrastructure elements like storage capacity and downtime to secure workloads.

D. Shared Responsibility model is a security model which includes global infrastructure elements set in the AWS Acceptable Use Policy.

30. Billy is exploring effects of attempting unauthorized port scans on EC2, what should Billy know about unauthorized port scans on EC2?

A. AWS maintains internal bandwidth which exceeds the provider-supplied Internet bandwidth and helps to mitigate any unauthorized port scans.

B. The AWS Acceptable Use Policy (AUP) considers unauthorized port scans as violations and reports such violations by checking traffic with a source IP or MAC address.

C. The AWS Acceptable Use Policy which every customer is bound by holds them in violation of the policy if they are found performing unauthorized port scans.

D. AWS offers SSL-protected endpoints extending server authentication and also generates new SSH host keys which are ways of mitigating unauthorized port scans.

31. Amy wants to configure an EC2 security group to deny traffic, what should Amy know about configuring EC2 security groups?

A. An EC2 security group can only be configured to deny specific rules, and separate rules can be configured for inbound traffic only.

B. An EC2 security group can only be configured to allow default rules, and to deny specific rules.

C. An EC2 security group can only be configured to allow specific rules, not to deny any, and separate rules can be configured for outbound and inbound traffic.

D. An EC2 security group can be configured to allow and deny specific rules, and separate rules can be configured for outbound traffic only.

32. Which of the following statements is true?

A. Securing Data-At-Rest: Synchronous transfer of data over SSL. Securing Data-In-Transit: Encryption using AES-128 (For data stored in S3).

B. Securing Data-In-Transit: Asynchronous transfer of data over SSL. Securing Data-At-Rest: Encryption using AES-256 (For data stored in S3).

C. Securing Data-In-Transit: Synchronous transfer of data over SSL. Securing Data-At-Rest: Encryption using AES-128 (For data stored in S3).

D. Securing Data-At-Rest: Asynchronous transfer of data over SSL. Securing Data-In-Transit: Encryption using AES-256 (For data stored in S3).

33. How should Access Keys be stored?

A. Dos for storing Access Keys: If you have a large fleet of EC3 instances, use User roles as a secure way of distributing keys.

B. Dos for storing Access Keys: If you have a large fleet of EC2 instances embed keys in your code.

C. Dos for storing Access Keys: If you have a large fleet of EC3 instances embed keys in your code and approved by account owner.

D. Dos for storing Access Keys: If you have a large fleet of EC2 instances, use IAM roles as a secure way of distributing keys.

34. How are EBS volumes and snapshots encrypted?

A. EBS volumes and snapshots are encrypted using SSH private keys, ensuring security while data moves between EC2 and EBS.

B. EBS volumes and snapshots are encrypted using AES-256 which encrypts data on servers hosting EC2 instances, ensuring security while data moves between EC2 and EBS.

C. EBS volumes and snapshots are encrypted by obtaining the administrator password using the private key and then signing is with RDP, ensuring security while data moves between EC2 and EBS.

D. EBS volumes and snapshots are encrypted using RSA keys, ensuring security while data moves between EC2 and EBS.

# 13

# Risk Management and Compliance

1. Which of the following statements is true?

   A. Ways in which AWS educates customers about AWS security and control environment: By supplying certificates, reports, etc. directly to account owners.

   B. Ways in which AWS educates customers about AWS security and control environment: By storing certificates, reports, etc. and providing them directly to account owners.

   C. Ways in which AWS educates customers about AWS security and control environment: By supplying certificates, reports, etc. directly to customers.

   D. Ways in which AWS educates IAM users about AWS security and control environment: By supplying certificates, reports, etc. directly to customers.

2. Which of the following statements is true?

   A. Steps to Achieve Strong Compliance and Governance in AWS: * Identify and keep record of all 3rd party owned controls. * Ensure all control objectives are met.

   B. Steps to Achieve Strong Compliance and Governance in AWS: * Identify and keep record of all 3rd party owned controls. * Ensure all logical objectives are met.

   C. Steps to Achieve Strong Compliance and Governance in AWS: * Store and Record all Account owner owned controls. * Ensure all control objectives are met.

   D. Steps to Achieve Strong Compliance and Governance in AWS: * Identify and keep record of all IAM users owned controls. * Ensure all industry best practices are met.

3. Which of the following is an AWS Global Geographic region?

   A. Asia Pacific (Maldives).

   B. Asia Pacific (Malaysia).

   C. South America (Sao Paulo).

D. China (Shanghai).

4. What is the Shared Responsibility model?

  A. Shared Responsibility model is a security model which includes global infrastructure elements set in the AWS Acceptable Use Policy.
  B. Shared Responsibility model is a security model which includes global infrastructure elements like storage capacity and downtime to secure workloads.
  C. Shared Responsibility model is a security model used by AWS where AWS ensures security of the cloud infrastructure, and requires customers to secure workloads deployed in their AWS accounts.
  D. Shared Responsibility model is a security model used by AWS where AWS ensures availability of the cloud infrastructure, and requires customers to scale workloads deployed in their AWS accounts.

5. Which of the following is a prominent compliance certification of AWS?

  A. ISO 9002.
  B. ISO 27002.
  C. FIPS 140-2.
  D. PCI DSS (Level 3).

6. Which of the following is a way in which AWS provides IT Control Information to customers?

  A. Specific control definition.
  B. Primary control standard compliance.

C. Key controls standard compliance.
  D. Key control definition.

7. What is the number of geographic regions that AWS Cloud operates from?

  A. 12
  B. 16
  C. 42
  D. 40

8. Which of the following is a step to achieve strong compliance and governance in AWS?

  A. Step 1: Archive and retrieve control objectives that are in line with industry requirements.
  B. Step 1: Review all available information about the IT controls, and store all compliance requirements.
  C. Step 1: Review and record control requirements that are in line with 3rd party owned requirements.
  D. Step 1: Review all available information about the IT environment, and document all compliance requirements.

9. What is the Shared Responsibility in AWS IT controls?

  A. Shared responsibility in AWS is extended to IT controls which includes global infrastructure elements set in the AWS Acceptable Use Policy.
  B. Shared responsibility in AWS is extended to IT controls where AWS ensures security of the cloud infrastructure, and requires customers to secure workloads deployed in their AWS accounts.

C. Shared responsibility in AWS is extended to IT controls where the management, operation, and verification of IT controls is done with AWS handling controls for physical infrastructure, and customer managing those for guest OS's.

D. Shared responsibility in AWS is extended to IT controls where AWS includes global infrastructure elements like storage capacity and downtime to secure workloads.

10. Which of the following describes a way in which AWS educates customers about AWS security and control environment?

   A. By offering functionalities, services etc. directly to customers.

   B. By acquiring industry standard certifications and 3rd party attestations.

   C. By supplying certificates, reports, etc. directly to account owners.

   D. By acquiring industry standard certifications and account owner attestation.

11. Which of the following is a step to achieve strong compliance and governance in AWS?

   A. Archive and retrieve control objectives that are in line with industry requirements.

   B. Review and record control requirements that are in line with 3rd party owned requirements.

   C. Review all available information about the IT controls, and store all compliance requirements.

D. Devise and enforce control objectives that are in line with compliance requirements.

12. What is an AWS Business Risk Plan?

   A. AWS Business Risk Plan is a plan developed by the AWS risk management team that identifies key risk areas and intimates the account managers.

   B. AWS Business Risk Plan is a plan developed by the account managers to identify common risks and ensure smooth functioning of operations.

   C. AWS Business Risk Plan is a plan developed by the AWS risk management team that identifies risks and enforces controls to manage/mitigate them.

   D. AWS Business Risk Plan is a plan developed by the AWS development team that identifies threats and enforces how to control them.

13. Which of the following can be considered as a core area of the AWS Risk and Compliance Program?

   A. Business continuity planning

   B. Information management

   C. Disaster recovery

   D. Risk management

14. What are the characteristics of IT Governance in AWS?

   A. IT Governance in AWS involves alignment of operations and productivity across the physical environment.

B. IT Governance in AWS is where the customer is responsible for maintaining proper governance across the IT control environment, irrespective of the deployment type (cloud/on-premises/hybrid).

C. IT Governance in AWS implies that account owner is responsible for maintaining proper governance across AWS services and implementing best practices.

D. IT Governance in AWS im-plies that customer is responsible for maintaining configured resources correctly and auditing reports and making sure services are compliant.

15. Which of the following is a component of AWS Control Environment?

A. IT Operations.

B. Security Groups.

C. Technology.

D. Configurations.

# 14

## Architectural Best Practices

1. Which of the following statements is true?

   A. Stateless Applications are applications which require information on past interactions, and store session data.

   B. Stateless Applications are applications which require no parameters on past interactions, and do not rely on session data.

   C. Stateful Applications are applications which require no information on past interactions, and do not store session data.

   D. Stateless Applications are applications which require no information on past interactions, and do not store session data.

2. Which of the following statements is true?

   A. List of AWS Architecture Best Practices: * Designing for security processes. * Decoupling elasticity.

   B. List of AWS Architecture Best Practices: * Design-ing for parallelization * Decoupling application components.

   C. List of AWS Architecture Best Practices: * Designing for failure. * Decoupling application components.

   D. List of AWS Architecture Best Practices: * Designing for integrity. * Decoupling security components.

3. How can building a highly available architecture on AWS be achieved?

   A. A Highly available architecture on AWS can be achieved by building systems that can withstand the failure of single or multiple components.

   B. A Highly available architecture on AWS can be achieved by building processes that ensure confidentiality and integrity of resources.

   C. A Highly available architecture on AWS can be achieved by building systems that do not violate the AWS Acceptable Use policy.

D. A Highly available architecture on AWS can be achieved by building systems that are operationally effective of IT controls.

4. What are the characteristics of Active Redundancy?

    A. Active Redundancy uses the failover process to recover functionality on a secondary resource when a resource fails, and causes downtime during the failover process.

    B. Active Redundancy uses the failover process to recover functionality on a primary resource when a resource fails, and causes no downtime during the failover process.

    C. Active Redundancy distributes requests to active resources so that if a resource fails, others can take on the extra workload.

    D. Active Redundancy distributes requests to multiple redundant resources so that if a resource fails, others can take on the extra workload, and causes no downtime.

5. Which of the following is a benefit of Bootstrapping?

    A. You can quickly recreate Internet-scale applications with less effort.

    B. You can quickly recreate environments with less effort.

    C. Minimize human-induced controls in datasets.

    D. Minimize human-induced errors in scaling.

6. What are the characteristics of Vertical Scaling?

    A. Vertical Scaling cannot work beyond certain limits, and hence is not a highly available or cost-effective way.

    B. Vertical Scaling is allowed for stateful applications which can fully utilize the elasticity of cloud computing.

    C. Vertical Scaling can work beyond certain limits, and hence is a highly available and a cost-effective way.

    D. Vertical Scaling is allowed for Internet-scale applications which can fully utilize the elasticity of cloud computing.

7. What is Loose Coupling?

    A. Loose Coupling is the practice of coupling system components so that they depend on each other directly.

    B. Loose Coupling is the practice of coupling system components as loosely as possible to reduce interdependencies, which in turn prevents failure of other components when one fails.

    C. Loose Coupling is the practice of coupling system components which are highly dependent on each other and components assume multiple responsibilities.

    D. Loose Coupling is the practice of coupling AWS services and refers to the approach of interconnecting services.

8. Which of the following is an IT architecture scaling option?

    A. Dynamic Scaling.

    B. Standby Scaling.

C. Active Scaling.

D. Vertical Scaling.

9. Which of the following is a benefit of Bootstrapping?

A. Retain more control over your resources.

B. Build a self-discoverable and self-healing Internet-scale application with elasticity of cloud computing.

C. Build a highly available and self-healing IT applications with increased resistance to failover.

D. Retain more control over your operations.

10. What are the characteristics of Elastic Architecture?

A. Elastic Architecture is an IT architecture that supports increase in failover, storage options, or users, without a dip in performance.

B. Elastic Architecture is an IT architecture that supports increase in traffic, data size, or users, without a dip in performance.

C. Elastic Architecture is an IT architecture that supports increase in resources, bucket size, or components, without a dip in performance.

D. Elastic Architecture is an IT architecture that supports increase in scaling, data interaction, or computing, without a dip in performance.

11. What does leveraging different storage options imply?

A. Leverage Different Storage Options is the practice of recreating environments (from several options offered by AWS) to suit different types of applications, to optimize Internet-scale applications.

B. Leverage Different Storage Options is the practice of self-discoverable options (from several resources offered by AWS) to suit different types of infrastructure, to optimize performance and save costs.

C. Leverage Different Storage Options is the practice of choosing different options (from several storage options offered by AWS) to suit different types of datasets, to optimize performance and save costs.

D. Leverage Different Storage Options is the practice of choosing different options (from several storage options offered by AWS) to suit different types of components, to self-heal IT environments.

12. Which of the following statements is true?

A. Standby Redundancy uses the failover process to recover functionality on a secondary resource when a resource fails, and causes downtime during the failover process.

B. Standby Redundancy uses the failover process to route functionality on an active resource when a resource fails, and causes downtime during the failover process.

C. Standby Redundancy uses the redundant process to recover functionality on a dynamically available resource when a resource fails, and causes no downtime during the failover process.

D. Active Redundancy uses the failover process to recover functionality on a secondary resource when a resource fails, and causes downtime during the failover process.

13. How can Horizontal Scaling be achieved?

A. Horizontal Scaling can be achieved by increasing the specifications of individual resources.

B. Horizontal Scaling can be achieved by increasing the number of stateless applications.

C. Horizontal Scaling can be achieved by increasing the number of users.

D. Horizontal Scaling can be achieved by increasing the number of resources.

# 15

# Answers To Introduction

1. Which of the following statements is true?
   Answer: A

   AWS Regions are physical geographic locations with a cluster of data centers that enable deployment of data in multiple locations around the globe.

2. Which of the following statements is true?
   Answer: C

   Ways in which AWS educates customers about AWS security and control environment: By supplying certificates, reports, etc. directly to customers.

3. Which of the following statements is true?
   Answer: B

   Amazon S3 Common Use Cases include: * Backup and archive * Big data analytics * Disaster Recovery

4. Which of the following is an advantage of Cloud Computing?
   Answer: D

   Global in minutes

5. Jack wants to use a Management Tool offered by AWS, what tool should Jack use?
   Answer: B

   AWS CloudTrail

6. What is the characteristic of an Internal load balancer in ELB?
   Answer: A

   Internal load balancer balances load between the tiers of a multi-tier application. E.g. Routes traffic to EC2 instances in VPCs with private subnets.

7. Which of the following statements is true?
   Answer: C

   List of AWS Architecture Best Practices: * Designing for failure. * Decoupling application components.

8. Which of the following statements is true?
   Answer: C

   IAM enables granular level control over the people and applications that can access an AWS account.

9. How can building a highly available architecture on AWS be achieved?
   Answer: A

A Highly available architecture on AWS can be achieved by building systems that can withstand the failure of single or multiple components.

10. Which of the following is a primary cloud computing deployment model?
Answer: C

Hybrid Deployment

11. Which of the following statements is true?
Answer: C

List of Database Services offered by AWS: Amazon RDS Amazon DynamoDB Amazon Redshift

12. What is the characteristic of an Internet-facing load balancer in ELB?
Answer: D

Internet-facing load balancer in ELB takes requests from clients over the Internet, and allocates them to EC2 instances registered with the load balancer.

13. Which of the following statements is true?
Answer: B

List of Storage and Content Delivery services offered by AWS: Amazon S3 Amazon Glacier Amazon EBS

14. What is a Maintenance Window?
Answer: C

Maintenance Window is the 60 minute time duration specified by the customer when either requested or required software patching occurs in Amazon ElastiCache.

15. Which of the following statements is true?
Answer: D

Security Standards and Certifications AWS is in compliance with: * FISMA * DIACAP * ISO 9001, ISO 27001, and ISO 27018

16. Which of the following statements is true?
Answer: A

Benefits of AZs: Low-latency, cost-effective connectivity to other AZs within a region.

17. Which of the following statements is true?
Answer: B

Hybrid model is an architectural pattern that connects infrastructure and applications between existing resources not located in the cloud and the cloud-based resources.

18. Which of the following describes a way in which AWS educates customers about AWS security and control environment?
Answer: B

By acquiring industry standard certifications and 3rd party attestations.

19. Which of the following is a Security and Identity service offered by AWS?
Answer: A

AWS IAM

20. Which of the following statements is true?
Answer: B

You can integrate CloudHSM with Amazon RDS only for Oracle instances, allowing AWS to operate Oracle databases while you still control master encryption keys.

21. Meg wants to access AWS cloud services platform, How should Meg access the services?
Answer: C

You can access AWS cloud services platform using one of these: AWS management console AWS Command Line Interface (CLI) AWS Software Development Kits (SDKs)

22. Which of the following statements is true?
Answer: D

List of Application Services offered by AWS: Amazon API Gateway Amazon Elastic Transcoder Amazon SNS

23. What is All-in Deployment Model?
Answer: C

All-in Deployment Model is an application that is completely deployed in the cloud, with all its components running in the cloud.

24. What is Amazon S3?
Answer: C

Amazon S3 is the core object storage service on AWS that offers unlimited data storage and high durability.

25. Which of the following is an advantage of Cloud Computing?
Answer: A

Economies of scale

*16*

# Answers To Content Storage

1. Which of the following statements is true?
   Answer: A

   Performing a GET on an object with a delete marker returns a 404 error and an 'x-amz-delete-marker: true' header.

2. Which of the following describes the permission contexts which are evaluated for account owners and IAM users when they perform an operation on an S3 object?
   Answer: B

   Permission contexts evaluated for both account owners and IAM users when they perform an operation on an S3 object: User context Bucket context Object context

3. What is the Maximum expiration for a pre-signed S3 URL?
   Answer: C

   Multiple years

4. Ida wants to know how to encrypt Amazon S3 data, how should Ida attempt S3 Encryption?
   Answer: B

   Either server-side or client-side encryptions can be used for data

stored on S3, with Amazon KMS managing the encryption keys.

5. Which of the following describes the permission context which is evaluated when an account owner performs an operation on an S3 bucket owned by the owner?
   Answer: B

   Bucket context

6. Which of the following statements is true?
   Answer: A

   A bucket policy can control access to specific S3 objects.

7. Which of the following statements is true?
   Answer: B

   Amazon S3 Common Use Cases include: * Backup and archive * Big data analytics * Disaster Recovery

8. What are the characteristics of Amazon Server Access Logs?
   Answer: A

   Amazon Server Access logs are enabled to track requests sent to an S3 bucket and provide details like the requestor, time, object, action, response, etc.

9. Mia wants to know how to delete objects permanently when the versioning is on, how should Mia attempt this?
Answer: D

Permanent deletion of an object is possible even when versioning is enabled if the version ID is included in the DELETE request.

10. Which of the following is a best practice to maximize the performance of S3?
Answer: B

Use CloudFront

11. Which of the following is a step to enable Static Web Hosting on S3?
Answer: D

Create a bucket with the website hostname.

12. Which of the following statements is true?
Answer: D

AWS regions for the S3 buckets can be chosen by the customers and data will be stored in that region unless a customer explicitly copies it to a different region.

13. Which of the following describes a valid option to implement S3 encryption?
Answer: A

Client-side encryption with KMS-managed keys .

14. What is the use of prefix and delimiter parameters?
Answer: B

Prefixes and Delimiters are used in listing key names.

15. Which of the following describes a countermeasure for the poor performance caused by S3 access patterns?
Answer: B

Using CloudFront to reduce load.

16. Noe was searching for the creation of one-time pre-signed S3 download links, what should Noe know about the creation of the download links?
Answer: D

It is not possible to create a one-time pre-signed S3 download link, but a pre-signed URL with a very short expiration can be created.

17. Amy is facing a partial upload failure of a single part of a multipart S3, how can Amy resolve this situation?
Answer: B

If a single part of a multipart S3 upload fails, it is possible to retry the upload of that part by specifying the part number.

18. What is Object Storage?
Answer: B

Object Storage is a type of data storage in which the data is managed as objects that comprise both data and metadata, manipulated by an API.

19. Which of the following describes a Bucket owner's rights on objects not owned by them?
Answer: D

If an object in a bucket is not owned by the bucket owner, the owner: Can deny access to it

20. What is a Cross-region replication?
Answer: A

Cross-region replication is a feature that allows asynchronous replication of new objects from a source bucket in an AWS region to a target bucket in a different region.

21. Which of the following statements is true?
Answer: B

Mechanisms to secure S3 data are: * Strong bucket policies * MFA delete and versioning * Creating a separate account to store objects and using cross-account access

22. Which of the following is a step to retrieve an archive for Glacier?
Answer: D

Initiate an archive retrieval job.

23. Which of the following describes the permission context that is evaluated when an IAM user performs an operation on an S3 bucket, owned by its parent account?
Answer: D

Permission context evaluated when an IAM user performs an operation on an S3 bucket that is owned by its parent account: User context

24. Which of the following best describes who can be granted controlled access to Amazon S3 objects?
Answer: C

Controlled access may be granted to anyone using S3 bucket policies, ACLs, and AWS IAM.

25. Which of the following best describes a use case of an Amazon S3 storage class?
Answer: D

Amazon S3 Standard: For general purpose data that requires high performance and low latency.

26. Ben is an account owner who wants to grant Tom, another account owner access to an S3 resource, can Tom grant access of the same resource to some other owner?
Answer: A

Recipient of delegated permission can only further delegate permission to users in their account and not to the owner of a different AWS account.

27. What is a Multipart Upload API?
Answer: C

Multipart Upload API is the API that allows for large objects to be copied/uploaded as a set of parts, providing better network utilization, and the ability to pause and resume.

28. Which of the following statements is true?
Answer: D

S3 supports bucket policies where all objects in a bucket can be mandated to use server-side encryption.

29. What are the characteristics of Vaults in Amazon Glacier?
Answer: C

Vaults are containers for archives and an AWS account can have upto 1,000 vaults with each vault storing unlimited number of archives.

30. What can you expect when an S3 object's expiration policy is triggered and the versioning is not on?
Answer: A

When the versioning is not on, the object is deleted.

31. How is the storage partition of objects determined in S3?
Answer: D

The storage partition of objects in S3 is determined by the string values of the object key names which are stored alphabetically as an index.

32. What are the characteristics of Pre-signed URLs?
Answer: A

Pre-Signed URLs protect media and other web content against unauthorized web scraping by granting time-limited permissions to download objects.

33. What is the data consistency model that is employed by Amazon S3?
Answer: A

Amazon S3 offers eventual data consistency for overwrite PUTs and Deletes, and for PUTs of new objects it provides read-after-write consistency.

34. What are the characteristics of Range GETs?
Answer: B

Range GETs allows users to download (GET) only the required portion of an object instead of having to download the entire object.

35. Rex is exploring spike in S3 request rates, what should Rex do when there is a very large and sudden spike in request rates?
Answer: B

When very large spikes in S3 requests rates are expected, a support case can be submitted to Amazon so they can prepare for the extra load.

36. What is the encryption level of S3 objects?
Answer: C

All S3 objects are encrypted with a unique key at the object level, and not the bucket level.

37. Which of the following statements is true?
Answer: C

Replicated: Objects encrypted (server-side) using Amazon S3 managed encryption keys, and their versions.

38. What should the byte range be for range retrievals in Glacier?
Answer: D

The byte range should begin at 0 or any 1MB interval thereafter, and end at the end of the archive or any 1MB interval greater than the beginning range.

39. How is a Key defined?
Answer: C

Key is a unique identifier that identifies every S3 object in a bucket, and can be upto 1024 bytes of Unicode UTF-8 characters like embedded slashes, backslashes, etc.

40. Which of the following statements is true?
Answer: B

Best practices to maximize S3 performance: * Use CloudFront * Use multipart PUTs to maximize bandwidth

41. What are the characteristics of Amazon S3 Versioning?
Answer: D

S3 technology keeps multiple retrievable versions of all objects (marked with unique version IDs) to protect data against malicious or accidental deletion.

42. Gia is searching for multi-factor authentication used by S3 server-side encryption, what safeguards are used to protect the data at rest?
Answer: C

S3 server-side encryption uses AES-256 block cipher that encrypts each object with a unique key, and each key with a master key that is regularly rotated.

43. Eva is searching for encryption of object metadata, what should Eva know about S3 server-side encryption on object metadata?
Answer: A

S3 only provides server-side encryption of the objects in the bucket, not the metadata.

44. What is Block Storage?
Answer: B

Block Storage is a type of data storage in which the data is managed at device level as addressable blocks.

45. What operations are protected by MFA Delete?
Answer: B

Permanent deletion of an object version.

46. What is not replicated by Amazon S3?
Answer: D

Not replicated: Objects encrypted (server-side) using customer provided or AWS KMS managed encryption keys.

47. What is the key characteristic of Amazon Glacier?
Answer: D

Archives are identified by system-generated archive IDs.

48. Which of the following statements is true?
Answer: B

With delegated permission, a user can modify a policy on a bucket in another AWS account.

49. What can you expect if the Versioning is set on or is suspended?
Answer: C

Versioning on/suspended: Current version of the object is made non-current by adding a delete marker; and all non-current versions are saved.

50. Which of the following describes a countermeasure for the poor performance caused by S3 access patterns?
Answer: B

Reversing key names.

51. Ron wants to know how the S3 bucket policies are applied to API calls, what are the credentials used for the S3 bucket policies?
Answer: D

In Amazon S3, bucket policies applied to API calls are written with the credentials of the account owner.

52. Which of the following statements is true?
Answer: B

It is possible to use cross-region replication in S3 to replicate objects from a bucket in one AWS account to a bucket in another AWS account.

53. What is the characteristic of the Object Lifecycle Management?
Answer: D

Object Lifecycle Management enables automatic transitioning of data between storage classes and even data deletion based on time.

54. Which of the following statements is true?
Answer: D

Amazon Glacier: For archives and long-term backups that are seldom accessed (offers high durability and a retrieval time of 3 to 5 hours)

55. Which of the following statements is true?
Answer: C

The largest archive that can be uploaded onto a Glacier archive in a single upload request cannot be more than 4GB in size.

56. How much time does it take for a retrieval job to be completed on Glacier?
Answer: D

It takes 3 to 5 hours to for a retrieval job to be completed on Glacier.

57. What is the maximum size for S3 objects that can be downloaded through BitTorrent?
Answer: A

The maximum size of BitTorrent downloadable objects is 5 GB.

58. What is Amazon Glacier?
Answer: D

Amazon Glacier is a low-cost storage service with secure, durable, and flexible storage solutions for online backup and data archiving.

59. Which of the following statements is true?
Answer: D

Amazon Glacier supports multipart uploads, and it is recommended for archives over 100MB in size.

60. Which of the following describes the ordering of the response from S3 GET Bucket operation?
Answer: D

The operation in S3 which returns a list of key names sequenced alphabetically.

61. What are the characteristics of Amazon S3 Event notifications?
Answer: D

Event notifications are set up at bucket level to send responses (like Amazon SQS/SNS messages or trigger a Lambda function) to create/delete actions taken on objects stored in S3.

# 17

## Answers To Compute and Block Storage

1. What is AMI?
   Answer: B

   AMI defines the initial software state of an instance at the time of launch including OS and configuration, initial state of patches, and application/system software.

2. Which of the following describes what the R3 Instance Type is best suited for?
   Answer: C

   Distributed memory caches

3. Eli is trying to detach an EC2 instance's primary ENI, how should Eli attempt detaching the Primary ENI of an EC2 Instance?
   Answer: B

   The Primary ENI cannot be detached from an EC2 instance, but you can create additional ENIs and attach them to the instance.

4. How can you launch an EC2 Instance?
   Answer: C

   You can launch an Amazon EC2 instance by specifying an AMI and an instance type.

5. Which of the following is a characteristic of a Security Group Rule?
   Answer: C

   Deny by default

6. What are Instances?
   Answer: A

   Instances are virtual servers through the launching of which Amazon EC2 helps acquire your required compute, Amazon charges you on an hourly basis for the use of instances.

7. What are the data transfer charges between instances in different AZs?
   Answer: B

   If you are transferring data from an instance in one AZ to an instance in another, you will be charged out for the former and in for the latter.

8. What is the maximum number of accumulated CPU credits for the instance type T2.medium of the T2 (burstable) server class?
   Answer: C

   24 hours of credits. Which means: T2.micro - 144 (6 CPU Credits/hr * 24) T2.small - 288 (12 CPU Credits / hr * 24) T2.medium - 576 (24 CPU Credits / hr * 24)

9. Which of the following statements is true?
Answer: D

EC2 Instance Profile is a container for IAM roles which can be used to associate roles to an EC2 instance at instance start-up.

10. What is the default maximum number of EC2-Classic security groups per instance?
Answer: C

500

11. Which of the following describes what the T2 (burstable) server class is best suited for?
Answer: D

Development environments

12. Which of the following describes a modification that can be done on an existing RI?
Answer: B

Changing instance type within an instance family.

13. What are Instance Stores?
Answer: B

Instance Stores are temporary block storage located on physically attached disks on the host computer, included with the hourly cost of your instance.

14. Which of the following statements is true?
Answer: D

Spot Instances can be used to alleviate traffic in a workload where many Reserved Instances are reading from a queue.

15. Which of the following EC2 instance type is storage optimized?
Answer: C

I2

16. Which of the following statements is true?
Answer: D

EIPs can be attached to the ENI's private IP addresses, and you can also attach one EIP with each private IP address.

17. What is an ENI?
Answer: A

ENI is a virtual network interface that can be attached to an instance in a VPC.

18. What is the best Instance type for Larger deployments of SAP, Microsoft SharePoint and other enterprise applications?
Answer: A

R3

19. What is the characteristic of a D2 Instance Type?
Answer: B

D2 Instance Type offers lowest price per disk throughput performance.

20. Ann wants to configure the Reverse DNS record for an Elastic IP, how should Ann attempt this?
Answer: A

Reverse DNS record for an EIP can be configured by filling out a form and ensuring that a corresponding forward DNS record directing to the EIP address exists.

21. What is a Default Security Group?
Answer: C

A VPC comes with a default security group which is attached to each EC2 instance that you launch, unless specified otherwise.

22. Which of the following statements is true?
Answer: B

ENI Attributes: A primary private IP address 1 or more secondary private IP addresses

23. Which of the following statements is true?
Answer: C

Recommendation for launching new EC2 placement group: Launch at once all instances you need, adding instances later may result in 'insufficient capacity' error.

24. Which of the following statements is true?
Answer: D

Accumulation of CPU Credits by T2 Instances: T2.micro: 6 credits per hour T2.small: 12 credits per hour T2.medium: 24 credits per hour

25. What is the CPU Credit for an EC2 burstable instance type?
Answer: C

The performance of a full core for 60 seconds.

26. What is Bootstrapping?
Answer: A

Bootstrapping provides a script to be run on an instance at launch to initialize it with OS configurations and applications.

27. Which of the following statements is true?
Answer: B

A placement group can span peered VPCs. But, full-bisection bandwidth might not be available between instances in peered VPCs in such a case.

28. Amy wants to change an RI from one instance family (c1.4xlarge) to another (m1.xlarge), How should Amy attempt this?
Answer: A

An RI is attached to a specific instance family for the entire RI term, and can't be reassigned from one instance family to another, unless it is a Linux/UNIX RI.

29. Sam wants to merge placement groups, how can Sam attempt this?
Answer: B

Placement groups cannot be merged, instead, terminate the instances in one group, and relaunch the same instances into the other group.

30. How can the Instance Metadata be obtained?
Answer: B

You can obtain Instance Metadata through an HTTP call to a specific IP address.

31. Which of the following is a characteristic of EC2 Placement Group?
Answer: D

Cannot span across AZs

32. What is the best Instance type for NoSQL databases, Data Warehousing, Hadoop, and Cluster File Systems?
Answer: A

I2

33. What is the best Instance type for Caching fleets, Small and mid-size databases, and data processing that needs extra memory?
Answer: C

M3/M4

34. Which of the following statements is true?
Answer: D

Instance Types that support Jumbo Frames (9001 MTU): Memory Optimized: R3 and CR1 Storage Optimized: HS1, HI1, D2 and I2

35. What are the capabilities of VM import/export?
Answer: B

EC2 allows you to import your existing virtual machines to AWS as instances or AMIs, and such imported instances can also be exported back to a virtual environment.

36. What is Compute?
Answer: D

Compute is the amount of computational power needed to achieve your workload.

37. What is EBS-Backed in the context of an EC2 instance?
Answer: C

EBS-Backed: Where an Amazon EBS volume (created from a snapshot) is the root device for an instance launched from the AMI.

38. Tom wants to move existing instances to placement groups, how should Tom attempt this?
Answer: C

Existing instances can't be moved to placement groups, but you can create an AMI from the instance, and launch a new instance from the AMI into a placement group.

39. What is default maximum number of EC2 reservations per region?
Answer: D

20 instance reservations/month per AZ

40. How can you interpret the effect of Security Groups?
Answer: C

All the rules of all the security groups apply on an instance that is a member of several security groups.

41. What is Instance Store Backed in the context of an EC2 instance?
Answer: C

Instance Store Backed: Where an instance store volume (created from a template saved in S3) is the root device for an instance launched from the AMI.

42. What is the characteristic of an I2 Instance Type?
Answer: C

I2 Instance Type offers high IOPS at low costs and provides high speed SSD-backed instance storage for very high random I/O performance.

43. How can you access a newly launched Linux instance?
Answer: B

Linux: Use the private half of the key pair to connect to the instance via SSH.

44. Which of the following is a benefit of EC2 Placement Groups?
Answer: D

High throughput

45. Which of the following describes what the C3/C4 Instance Type is best suited for?
Answer: B

Ad serving

46. Which of the following is a feature of an On-Demand Instance?
Answer: A

Highest per hour cost

47. Which of the following describes what the G2 Instance Type is best

suited for?
Answer: D

Machine learning

48. Which of the following is an EC2 Metric available in CloudWatch?
Answer: B

CPU credits

49. What is the characteristic of a C3/C4 Instance Type?
Answer: C

C3/C4 Instance Type offers a balance of memory, compute and network resources, and offers the lowest price/compute performance and highest performing processors.

50. What is the maximum number of RIs that can be purchased per AZ per month?
Answer: A

Up to 20 RIs can be purchased along with the EC2 APIs per month for every AZ. Any request for additional RIs will have to be submitted to Amazon via a form.

51. Which of the following is a benefit of Enhanced Networking?
Answer: A

Considerably higher PPS performance.

52. Emma wants to move an RI across a different AWS region, what should Emma know about moving RIs across regions?
Answer: D

RIs cannot be moved across different AWS regions as they are associated with a particular region for the entire term.

53. Greg wants to apply RI capacity reservations to instances launched with an EC2 Placement Group, what should Greg know about RI Capacity Reservations?
Answer: D

Capacity reservations of reserved instances do not apply to instances within an EC2 placement group. They apply for on-demand instances in an AZ.

54. Which of the following is a feature of a Reserved Instance?
Answer: C

Offer lower costs over the lifetime of reservation

55. Amy wants to configure an EC2 security group to deny traffic, what should Amy know about configuring EC2 security groups?
Answer: C

An EC2 security group can only be configured to allow specific rules, not to deny any, and separate rules can be configured for outbound and inbound traffic.

56. Lucy wants to use an existing ENI while creating new EC2 instance, how should Lucy attempt this?
Answer: D

You can use an existing ENI as the primary network interface to create a new instance by specifying the ENI to be attached for both primary and additional ENIs.

# 18

## Answers To Virtual Private Cloud

1. What is a customer gateway (CGW)?
   Answer: D

   A customer gateway is the anchor on your side of the connection, which can be software or a physical appliance.

2. Which of the following statements is true?
   Answer: A

   Amazon does not allow you to change the size of an existing VPC, and you can terminate the VPC and create a new one with the desired CIDR block.

3. Tim wants to connect multiple CGWs to a single VGW, what should Tim need to know about using CGWs with VGWs?
   Answer: D

   Amazon VPC allows you to connect multiple CGWs to a single VGW, or to connect a single router to multiple VGWs.

4. Which of the following statements is true?
   Answer: B

   Amazon VPC Public IP address is an AWS owned public IP address that can be automatically assigned to instances launched in a subnet.

5. What is the maximum number of VPN connections per VPC?
   Answer: C

   10

6. Which of the following statements is true?
   Answer: B

   VPC Optional Components: * IGWs * EIP addresses

7. Which of the following statements is true?
   Answer: B

   Endpoint is a VPC component that helps build a private connection between your VPC and another AWS service (in the same region) without needing access over the Internet.

8. What is a Subnet?
   Answer: A

   Subnets are segments of an Amazon VPC's IP address range, defined by CIDR blocks, where groups of isolated resources can be placed.

9. What is a Private Subnet?
   Answer: A

   Private Subnet is a subnet that doesn't have a route to the IGW.

10. What is a VPN CloudHub?
    Answer: C

    VPN CloudHub is an AWS service that lets you route between your on-premises networks using a VPG.

11. What is a VPN-only Subnet?
    Answer: B

    VPN-only Subnet is a subnet that doesn't have a route to the IGW, but has the traffic routed to a VPG.

12. What are the characteristics of a Network ACL?
    Answer: B

    A Network ACL is applied on a subnet level and the traffic is stateless.

13. What is Amazon VPC Peering?
    Answer: A

    Peering is a networking connection that, using a request/accept protocol, allows instances in 2 VPCs to communicate with each other like they are in the same network.

14. What is the default maximum number of active peering connections per VPC?
    Answer: D

    Maximum no. of active peering connections per VPC: 50

15. Jenny wants to remove the Deny All rule at the bottom of an NACL rule list, what does Jenny need to know about the default deny all rule?
    Answer: C

    Every network ACL has a rule at the bottom of the rule list identified by an asterisk, which denies a packet if it doesn't match any of the other rules.

16. Which of the following statements is true?
    Answer: C

    Smallest possible size for a VPC: 28 (16 addresses)

17. Which of the following statements is true?
    Answer: C

    ENI attributes: 1 public IP address A MAC address A source/destination check flag

18. Which of the following statements is true?
    Answer: C

    Amazon VPC does not support either multicast or broadcast.

19. Which of the following statements is true?
    Answer: B

    VPC Primary Components: * Subnets * Route tables

20. Which of the following statements is true?
    Answer: C

    The default network ACL of a VPC is configured to let all inbound and outbound traffic to flow to and from each subnet.

21. What is a DHCP Option set?
    Answer: A

    DHCP Option set is the component of Amazon VPC that helps you host name assignment to your own resources.

22. Which of the following statements is true?
    Answer: C

    You cannot restrict access between VPC subnets using route tables.

23. What is the default maximum number of VPC virtual private gateways per account per region?

Answer: B

Maximum no. of VPC virtual private gateways per account per region: 5

24. Which of the following statements is true?

Answer: B

You cannot use all the IP addresses you assign to a subnet as Amazon retains the first 4 and last 1 addresses of all subnets for IP networking uses.

25. Which of the following statements is true?

Answer: B

Maximum number of rules per security group: 50

26. Meg wants to reference security groups across the connection in peered VPCs, what should Meg know about referencing security groups?

Answer: A

Amazon VPC doesn't allow you to reference a security group from a peer VPC across the connection.

27. Which of the following statements is true?

Answer: B

A NAT instance or a NAT gateway allows instances in private subnets to launch outbound traffic to the Internet, enabling download, but blocking inbound traffic.

28. Susan wants to modify the default Deny All rule, what should Susan need to know about modification of the Deny All rule?

Answer: D

The default deny all rule cannot be removed or modified.

29. Susan wants to manually update route tables to route traffic across a VPC VPN link, what should Susan know about manually updating route tables?

Answer: A

If Route Propagation is not turned on, you can manually update route tables to route traffic across a VPC VPN link.

30. What is a Route Table?

Answer: A

Route Table is a set of rules that helps determine the direction of network traffic, and lets EC2 instances within the same VPC, but different subnets to communicate.

31. Which of the following statements is true?

Answer: B

Attributes of an ENI follow the ENI when it is attached/detached/reattached from and to instances.

# 19

# Answers To Load Balancing and Scaling

1. Which of the following is an ELB protocol that supports the Proxy Protocol?
   Answer: D

   TCP

2. Which of the following is an aspect that ELB allows to configure of the load balancer?
   Answer: A

   Proxy Protocol

3. How can you get a history of ELB API calls?
   Answer: D

   You can get a history of the API calls made on your account by turning on CloudTrail in your AWS Management Console.

4. What is the characteristic of an Internal load balancer in ELB?
   Answer: A

   Internal load balancer balances load between the tiers of a multi-tier application. E.g. Routes traffic to EC2 instances in VPCs with private subnets.

5. Which of the following statements is true?
   Answer: C

   Benefits of ELB Cross-Zone Load Balancing: Enhances an application's capacity to withstand the loss of one or more back-end instances.

6. Which of the following statements is true?
   Answer: D

   The Amazon CloudWatch log data is stored for 10 years for you to retrieve and use.

7. What is Elastic Load Balancing?
   Answer: C

   Elastic Load Balancing is a highly available AWS compute service that enables greater fault tolerance levels by distributing traffic across a group of EC2 instances in one or multiple AZs.

8. Which of the following statements is true?
   Answer: C

   If EC2 instances are healthy, the ELB Health Check status returns as InService, and if not, it returns as OutOfService.

9. What is the characteristic of an Internet-facing load balancer in

ELB?

Answer: D

Internet-facing load balancer in ELB takes requests from clients over the Internet, and allocates them to EC2 instances registered with the load balancer.

10. What is a common use case for Amazon CloudWatch?

Answer: B

In an application tier, you can decide when to add or remove EC2 instances by monitoring CPU utilization using CloudWatch.

11. Which of the following is a use case for Amazon CloudWatch?

Answer: B

Auto Scaling can be used to: Minimize costs by decreasing the number of running EC2 instances during troughs/demand dulls.

12. Which of the following is a step to create an SSL certificate for ELB?

Answer: B

Create an RSA private key and a CSR

13. What is Amazon CloudWatch?

Answer: D

Amazon CloudWatch is a tool that helps monitor resources by collecting and tracking metrics, creating notification alarms, and modifying monitored resources as per client defined rules.

14. Which of the following statements is true?

Answer: C

For front-end connections: Configured with a protocol and a port; client to load balancer.

15. How does the Amazon CloudWatch Log work?

Answer: D

How it works: Once you install a CloudWatch Log Agent on your EC2 instance, it collects log information and sends it back to CloudWatch.

16. Which of the following is a type of Amazon CloudWatch monitoring?

Answer: D

Basic

17. Tom wants to same multiple SSL certificates on an ELB, what should Tom know about storing SSL certificates on ELB?

Answer: A

You cannot save more than one SSL certificate on an ELB.

18. Which of the following statements is true?

Answer: C

You can use a self-signed certificate to terminate SSL on an ELB.

19. Which of the following TCP port is supported for ELB?

Answer: A

Port 25

20. What is Auto Scaling?

Answer: D

Auto Scaling is an AWS service that lets customers define criteria based on which their Amazon EC2 capacity can be automatically scaled in or out.

21. Which of the following is a valid status for any instance in an ELB?

Answer: A

InService

22. Charlie wants to use ELB cross-zone load balancing, how much should Charlie pay for the inter-zone transfer between the load balancer and back-end instances?

Answer: B

If you have enabled cross-zone load balancing, there are no extra charges for inter-zone data transfer between back-end instances and the load balancer nodes.

23. Which of the following is a type of load balancer in ELB?
Answer: C

Internal load balancer

24. What are the characteristics of Amazon CloudWatch Detailed monitoring?
Answer: C

Detailed monitoring: Must be enabled; Charged; Sends data points every minute; Allows data aggregation.

25. What is the default ELB timeout for client and back-end connections?
Answer: D

60 seconds

26. Which of the following statements is true?
Answer: B

For back-end connections: Configured with a protocol and a port; load balancer to back-end instance.

27. Which of the following is an EC2 Metric available in CloudWatch?
Answer: B

CPU credits

28. What is the characteristic of an HTTPS load balancer in ELB?
Answer: B

HTTPS load balancer encrypts data between clients who initiate HTTPS sessions and a load balancer.

29. Bill wants to check the status of a particular instance in an ELB, what should Bill know about checking the status of a specific instance in an ELB?
Answer: C

ELB allows you to check the status of a particular instance.

30. Which of the following is a plan which can help control Auto Scaling performance?
Answer: D

Maintain Current Instant Levels

# 20

# Answers To Identity and Access Management

1. Which of the following statements is true?
   Answer: D

   Authorization is the process where IAM manages the access of individual principals, and determines the actions a principal can and cannot carry out by associating them with policies.

2. Amy is searching for an additional layer of security for sensitive API calls, what do you suggest Amy should use?
   Answer: D

   Use MFA for an additional layer of security for sensitive API calls.

3. Which of the following statements is true?
   Answer: D

   EC2 Instance Profile is a container for IAM roles which can be used to associate roles to an EC2 instance at instance start-up.

4. Which of the following statements is true?
   Answer: A

   Policy Components are: * Effect * Service * Action

5. What is an Identity Broker in the context of an IAM identity federation?
   Answer: C

   Identity Broker is a custom-developed application that enables users to access the AWS Management Console by authenticating against the local identity store.

6. Eva wants to switch to an IAM role by attempting to use an account owner's credentials, how do you suggest Eva switch to an IAM role?
   Answer: B

   To switch to an IAM Role use Temporary security credentials or IAM user credentials.

7. What is an Identity Provider?
   Answer: B

   Identity Provider is the entity that manages and grants permissions to users outside of AWS to access and use AWS resources.

8. Which of the following statements is true?
   Answer: C

   IAM enables granular level control

over the people and applications that can access an AWS account.

9. Which of the following best describes a way of handling multiple permissions?
   Answer: C

   Action not explicitly allowed by a policy is denied.

10. What is a Temporary Security Token?
    Answer: D

    Temporary Security Token is a token issued by the AWS STS to an authenticated actor who assumes a role, in order to access AWS cloud services for a specified period.

11. Which of the following is the maximum of IAM Users per AWS account?
    Answer: C

    5000

12. Sam is exploring why there is an immediate access denial for any application running on an EC2 instance that is attached to an IAM role, what is Sam attempting?
    Answer: D

    Deletion of IAM Roles when attached to EC2 instances.

13. Which of the following statements is true?
    Answer: C

    Groups cannot directly access AWS as they do not have security credentials of their own.

14. S3 buckets represent what kind of services?
    Answer: D

    Services supporting resource-based IAM policies.

15. Which of the following is an entity to which an IAM policy can be assigned?
    Answer: B

    Role

16. Which of the following statements is true?
    Answer: C

    An IAM group cannot be granted its own IAM role as there is no option of assigning policies to such roles.

17. Which of the following statements is true?
    Answer: D

    All policies are evaluated and by default, all requests that are made are denied.

18. Which of the following best describes what rotation of keys can secure?
    Answer: A

    IAM User Accounts

19. Which of the following statements is true?
    Answer: D

    IAM User is a constant account that can be controlled using IAM, created for people or applications to access an AWS account.

20. What is an Access Key and Session Token used to authenticate?
    Answer: D

    IAM principal

21. Which of the following best describes the number of access keys that can be assigned to an IAM user?
    Answer: D

    2

22. Which of the following best describes the use of conditions in AWS?
Answer: D

Conditions provide security to IAM user accounts by restricting client IP address ranges.

23. Which of the following statements is true?
Answer: A

AWS MFA uses an authentication device that generates random, single-use, six-digit codes.

24. Which of the following best describes a step performed by an Identity Broker?
Answer: C

Calls AWS federation endpoint to get a sign in token using temporary credentials.

25. Which of the following best describes a step in a key rotation?
Answer: D

Configure all applications to use the new key.

26. Which of the following is a step to create an SSO URL for Federated Users?
Answer: A

Constructing a URL using the token from the federation endpoint.

27. Which of the following statements is true?
Answer: A

The three types of IAM principals are: * Root Users * IAM Users * Roles

28. Which of the following statements is true?
Answer: C

You cannot change the IAM Role on a Running Instance.

29. What is a Key Rotation?
Answer: B

Key Rotation is the process of regularly creating new access keys for IAM users in order to reduce security risks, where IAM allows two active keys to function at a time.

30. Which of the following statements is true?
Answer: B

Policies can be attached to IAM users directly or to an IAM group that the user is a member of.

31. How is a Root User defined?
Answer: A

Root User is the single sign-in principal associated with the actual AWS account with complete access which cannot be in any way restricted.

32. Which of the following describes a component of an IAM Request Context?
Answer: D

Calling principal

33. Which of the following describes how MFA works in AWS?
Answer: D

MFA is an authentication process that uses both a password (something you know) and a device generated OTP (something you have) to authenticate an AWS account.

34. Which of the following best describes a step performed by an Identity Broker?
Answer: D

Calls AWS STS to get user's temporary security credentials and permissions information.

35. Which of the following best describes a characteristic of Delegation?
Answer: B

Delegation is the process of granting of access rights for one AWS account to users in another AWS account.

36. Which of the following best describes an IAM group characteristic?
Answer: C

Permissions can be granted to groups using access control policies.

37. What is an IAM External ID?
Answer: C

IAM External ID is an identifier that can be granted to a third party in order for them to assume a role and access an AWS account.

38. Meg wants to access AWS resources and call MFA-protected APIs, how should Meg attempt this?
Answer: B

To access AWS resources and call MFA-protected APIs, Pass optional MFA parameters in the AWS STS API requests using temporary credentials.

39. Which of the following statements is true?
Answer: D

IAM roles common use case includes assigning privileges to an Amazon EC2 instance that can be assumed by the applications running on the particular instance.

40. Ken is working with the GetFederatedSession API that is MFA-protected and wants to pass MFA parameters, what should Ken know about API access for federated users?
Answer: B

MFA-protected API access does not work for federated users as the GetFederatedSession API does not accept MFA parameters.

41. Which of the following best describes the characteristics of IAM Users geography?
Answer: D

IAM Users are global entities that do not need a geographic region to be specified while defining user permissions.

42. Which of the following best describes an IAM user characteristic?
Answer: A

One user can be added to multiple groups.

43. Tia wants to protect access to specific AWS resources, how can Tia attempt this?
Answer: A

Use MFA to protect access to specific AWS resources.

44. Which of the following statements is true?
Answer: C

SAML can be used to allow federated users to access AWS APIs.

45. Which of the following is a common use case for an IAM role?
Answer: B

Consolidating identities from external IdPs.

46. Which of the following statements is true?
Answer: D

MFA authentication is enforced by attaching MFA related restrictions to IAM policies.

47. Which of the following statements is true?

Answer: C

There is no option of setting specific usage quota for individual IAM users; usage limits on the entire AWS account apply.

# 21

# Answers To Database Services

1. Which of the following is a benefit of Amazon Redshift?
   Answer: D

   Fast query performance through distributing records using columnar storage and parallelizing query execution across several compute nodes.

2. Which of the following is a use of the DynamoDB Cross regional table Copy AWS data pipeline?
   Answer: A

   Helps in disaster recovery during region failure or data loss.

3. Ann wants to configure Redshift to copy snapshots across regions, how should Ann attempt this?
   Answer: A

   Snapshots of Redshift clusters can be configured to be automatically copied to another AWS region, but it can only be copied to one destination region at a time.

4. Which of the following is a best practice to improve DynamoDB performance?
   Answer: C

   Make sure the keys are evenly allocated across partitions.

5. Which of the following is a benefit of Amazon Redshift?
   Answer: A

   Supports large databases by allowing scaling up or down of clusters using magnetic disk storage or SSD.

6. Which of the following is a condition that can trigger an automated failover of a Multi-AZ RDS Instance?
   Answer: A

   Change in the instance's storage type.

7. How can the disabling/enabling encryption on existing Redshift Clusters be attempted?
   Answer: B

   To disable/enable encryption on existing Redshift Clusters, unload data from the cluster and reload it to a new cluster with a preferred encryption setting.

8. What is Amazon DynamoDB?
   Answer: B

   Amazon DynamoDB is a completely managed database service that simplifies administration and operations for NoSQL databases providing low-latency and high scalability performance.

9. What is the default maximum number of RDS read replicas per master database?
Answer: D

5

10. Which of the following are options which are NOT available of RDS?
Answer: D

Accessing OS.

11. Which of the following is a best practice to improve DynamoDB performance?
Answer: C

Spread items across a fixed number of shards and attach a random shard identifier to shard writes of very hot tables.

12. Which of the following is a format of a NoSQL Database?
Answer: C

Document databases

13. Which of the following is an allowable RDS Storage Type?
Answer: A

Provisioned IOPS Storage

14. What is a Relational Database?
Answer: C

Relational Database is the most commonly used database type that offers a common interface where users can read/write from the database through queries/commands written using SQL.

15. Guy wants to manually initiate a failover for an RDS instance, how should Guy attempt this?
Answer: D

RDS automatically fails over an instance in many failure conditions,

and a manual failover can be done during reboot via an API call or the AWS Management Console.

16. Lou wants to use Standby Replicas for 'read traffic', what should Lou know about using standby replicas for 'read traffic'?
Answer: B

You cannot use Standby Replicas to serve 'Read Traffic' in RDS Multi-AZ deployments, but you will have to use a Read Replica.

17. Which of the following statements is true?
Answer: A

You can copy an automated RDS DB snapshot to create a manual snapshot in the same AWS region.

18. Tom wants to know whether restoring an RDS snapshot/point-in-time recovery have a new endpoint, what should Tom know about RDS Snapshot/Point-in-time Recovery?
Answer: A

The new DB instance created while restoring an RDS Snapshot or conducting an RDS point-in-time recovery will have a new endpoint.

19. Which of the following is a benefit of Amazon DynamoDB?
Answer: C

Creates tables in high speed to scale to an unlimited number of items.

20. Meg wants to increase storage and modify storage type on downtime, what should Meg know about increasing storage or modifying storage types?
Answer: A

Enhancing the allocated storage of an RDS instance doesn't result in outage/downtime, but changing the storage type to or from Magnetic Storage does.

21. How does Amazon RDS handle Multi-AZ failover?
Answer: D

The DNS change is handled by AWS automatically and the customer doesn't have to manually change the connection string, in the case of a Multi-AZ failover.

22. Which of the following statements is true?
Answer: B

Currently Redshift only supports Single-AZ deployments, and not Multi-AZ.

23. Which of the following describes how Redshift backs up data?
Answer: C

All data in a Redshift warehouse cluster is replicated at launch and also continuously and stored in Amazon S3.

24. Jo wants to copy DynamoDB table across regions using AWS Data Pipeline, what should Jo know about copying DynamoDB data in regions using the AWS data pipeline?
Answer: B

DynamoDB Cross Regional Table Copy AWS Data Pipeline template configures periodic copying of data between DynamoDB tables within or across AWS regions.

25. Ben wants to delete an RDS instance and wants to know whether Snapshots would be retained, what should Ben know about Snapshots of deleted RDS instances?
Answer: B

When an RDS instance is deleted, all manually created snapshots are retained and the automatic snapshots are deleted along with the instance.

26. What is the default maximum number of RDS instances per region?
Answer: B

40

27. Which of the following is a Database Engine that is supported by Amazon RDS?
Answer: B

Amazon Aurora

28. What is the default period of retention of RDS backups?
Answer: B

1 day

29. What is a Data Warehouse?
Answer: B

Data Warehouse is a central repository for data from one or many sources, used for complex querying, analysis, and report compilation via OLAP.

30. What would be the maximum size of a DynamoDB Item?
Answer: D

400 KB

31. Which of the following describes how Redshift backs up data?
Answer: A

Minimum of 3 copies of data is maintained: original, replica on compute nodes, and backup on S3.

32. Ed wants to know about effects of DB performance when backing up RDS Multi-AZ deployment, what should Ed know about RDS Multi-AZ deployment on DB performance?
Answer: C

Although the backup is taken from the standby instance in Multi-AZ DB deployments, some latency can still occur for both master and standby instances.

33. Pat wants to copy an RDS Snapshot across AWS regions, what should Pat know about copying RDS Snapshots?
Answer: A

Both automatic and manual snapshots of RDS instances can be copied from one AWS region to another.

34. What is the default maximum number of read and write capacity units per DynamoDB table?
Answer: A

10000 RCUs and 10000 WCUs

35. Which of the following is a type of workload for which Redshift would be better suited than RDS?
Answer: B

Workloads in which analytics can't interfere with OLTP

36. Which of the following is an AWS service that supports data loading to Redshift?
Answer: C

S3

37. What is the duration of RDS Multi-AZ Failover?
Answer: C

One to two minutes.

38. What is the maximum size of a result set returned by a DynamoDB query API call?
Answer: C

1 MB

39. Which of the following is a benefit of RDS?
Answer: D

RDS offers a consistent operational model for day-to-day administrative tasks.

40. Which of the following statements is true?
Answer: D

RDS Magnetic Storage is not a single-tenant service and is shared by DB instances of other customers which can cause variations in performance.

41. Which of the following statements is true?
Answer: B

AWS automatically fails over to a secondary RDS instance in a different AZ when the primary becomes unavailable, by pointing the DB endpoint to a new IP address.

# 22

# Answers To Events and Notifications

1. What is Receipt Handle in SQS?
Answer: C

Receipt Handle is a message response component that is needed while deleting the message or changing the message visibility.

2. What is an SWF Task List?
Answer: A

SWF Task List is an SWF feature that offers a flexible way of routing tasks to workers, and to organize different tasks of a workflow.

3. What is the characteristic of an SQS Access Control?
Answer: B

SQS Access Control enables assigning of policies to queues granting particular interactions to other accounts without needing that account to assume IAM roles from your account.

4. Which of the following is a batch operation that is supported by Amazon SQS?
Answer: A

ReceiveMessageBatch

5. Which of the following is an option that can specify Message Attributes in SQS?
Answer: C

AWS SDKs

6. Which of the following is a type of SNS client?
Answer: D

Publishers/producers

7. What is Fanout in SNS?
Answer: D

Fanout in SNS is the process of subscribing multiple SQS queues to a single SNS topic with the help of AMS Management Console.

8. What is Visibility Timeout in SQS?
Answer: D

Visibility Timeout in SQS is the period of time in which SQS makes a message unavailable for other components to receive/process as one component is already processing it.

9. What is the default maximum delay period for an SQS delay queue?
Answer: C

15 minutes

10. What is the characteristic of a Message Timer in SQS?
Answer: C

Message Timer is an SQS feature that lets you specify an initial period of invisibility for a message you've added in a queue.

11. What is the characteristic of an SQS Delay Queue?
Answer: B

SQS Delay Queue is a feature that lets you postpone delivery of messages in a queue for a defined period of time, making messages invisible to consumers for that delay period.

12. Which of the following is a defined operation for Amazon SQS queue?
Answer: D

ListQueue

13. What is an SQS Unique ID?
Answer: C

SQS Unique Id is a globally unique message ID that SQS returns when a message is delivered to the queue.

14. Amy wants to know whether it is possible to receive a message from an SQS queue more than once, what does Amy need to know about message delivery in SQS?
Answer: B

Although SQS is designed for 'at least once' message delivery, it is possible that messages are delivered multiple times.

15. What is a Dead Letter Queue in SQS?
Answer: C

Dead Letter Queue is an SQS supported queue that can be targeted by source queues to send messages which were not successfully processed.

16. What is Queue URL in SQS?
Answer: A

Queue URL is an identifier assigned by SQS to a queue which is unique within all your queues, and needs to be given every time you want to perform any action on that queue.

17. Which of the following statements is true?
Answer: D

Access to SQS is granted or denied only based on the AWS account, or a user created via AWS IAM.

18. What is the default maximum number of messages in an SQS queue?
Answer: A

Unlimited

19. Which of the following can be described as a common use of Amazon SQS?
Answer: B

Amazon SQS provides scalable and reliable storage for messages while they travel between servers.

20. Which of the following statements is true?
Answer: D

Message IDs cannot be more than 100 characters in length.

21. How does Long Polling work?
Answer: B

How it works: Sends a WaitTimeSeconds argument to ReceiveMessage of upto 20 seconds.

22. Which of the following statements is true?
Answer: A

DeleteMessage: Delete a specific message.

23. Which of the following is a type of programmatic actor that SWF interacts with?
Answer: B

Workflow starter

24. Which of the following is a component of a Message Attribute in SQS?
Answer: C

Data Type: String, Number, Binary

25. Which of the following is an Amazon SWF component?
Answer: A

Workflow history

26. What is a Message Attribute in SQS?
Answer: D

Message Attribute is a feature in SQS that allows you to provide structured metadata of messages which clients can use to better process messages.

27. Which of the following statements is true?
Answer: D

How Long Polling works: If there is no message in the queue, the call will wait for a message before returning upto WaitTimeSeconds.

28. Which of the following statements is true?
Answer: D

The maximum size of an SQS message also includes the message attributes (metadata).

29. What is Long Polling in SQS?
Answer: C

Long Polling is a feature that helps you reduce cost and the load on your client by reducing empty responses to messages and ousting false empty responses.

# 23

# Answers To DNS

1. Which of the following is a DNS resource record type that is supported by Amazon Route 53?
Answer: D

   A

2. Which of the following statements is true?
Answer: B

   Amazon Route 53 is a highly scalable and highly available authoritative DNS service by AWS that routes user requests to infrastructure on AWS like EC3 instances and ELB balancers.

3. Which of the following statements is true?
Answer: D

   Resolving name server sends this data to the user's browser to cache.

4. Which of the following is an Amazon Route 53 Weighted Routing Policy?
Answer: B

   Weighted Routing Policy: To route a percentage of traffic to a specific resource.

5. Which of the following statements is true?
Answer: A

   * Applications can be protected from regional outage by being deployed in multiple AWS regions.

6. What is a Route 53 Hosted Zone?
Answer: C

   A hosted zone is a compilation of resource record sets hosted by Amazon Route 53 that are managed under a single domain name.

7. Which of the following statements is true?
Answer: B

   Common routing policies: Simple Weighted Latency-based

8. Which of the following is a way in which an application can be built using Route 53 that is highly available and resilient?
Answer: A

   Health checks can make sure that applications delegate requests only to healthy EC2 instances.

9. Which of the following is a step involved in DNS resolution?
Answer: A

   Root server responds not with the answer, but with an address to a TLD server that has .com domain names information.

10. Which of the following is a record type in DNS?
Answer: C

SOA (Start of authority records)

11. What is IANA?
Answer: A

IANA is a body that controls a root zone database of all available TLDs.

12. What is Private DNS?
Answer: C

Private DNS is a feature offered by Route 53 that allows you to have authoritative DNS records within a VPC without disclosing those records to the Internet.

13. Which of the following is a step involved in DNS resolution?
Answer: A

Resolving server contacts the TLD server which provides the address for the RNS.

14. Which of the following statements is true?
Answer: B

There are many record types in DNS. E.g.: A (Address mapping records) NS (Name server records)

15. What is an Alias?
Answer: D

Alias is a records type in Route 53 that allows for the mapping of a zone apex DNS name to the account's ELB DNS name, or S3 website bucket or CloudFront distribution.

16. Which of the following is a step involved in DNS registration?
Answer: C

Domain names get individually registered in the central database - the WhoIS database.

17. Nick wants to associate multiple IP addresses to a single record, how should Nick attempt this?
Answer: C

With Route 53, multiple IP addresses can be listed for an A record to balance the load of geographically balanced web servers.

18. Bill wants to create a CNAME record at a zone apex, how should Bill attempt this?
Answer: A

Route 53 doesn't allow you to create a CNAME record at a zone apex which is the top node of a DNS namespace.

19. Which of the following is a step involved in DNS registration?
Answer: B

Domains are registered with domain registrars.

20. What is the time taken for DNS changes to propagate globally?
Answer: D

Amazon Route 53 propagates the updates made to DNS records within 60 seconds to its worldwide network of authoritative DNS servers.

21. Which of the following is an Amazon Route 53 Simple Routing Policy?
Answer: C

Simple Routing Policy: For when you have a single resource performing a given function for your domain.

22. What is a Wildcard Entry?
Answer: C

Wildcard Entry is a record in a DNS zone that will match requests for any domain name on the basis of the configurations set up by you.

*24*

# Answers To Caching

1. Which of the following statements is true?
   Answer: D

   ElastiCache upgrades a Memcached Cluster automatically if there is a need to protect against any security vulnerabilities.

2. What are the characteristics of Amazon ElastiCache?
   Answer: C

   Amazon ElastiCache offers cost-effective and scalable caching solutions for cloud applications, streamlining the launch and management of distributed in-memory caching environment.

3. Which of the following statements is true?
   Answer: D

   Benefits of In-Memory Caching: * Speeds up application's response time and enhances user experience.

4. What are the charges for ElastiCache Multi-AZ?
   Answer: B

   ElastiCache Multi-AZ feature is available free of charge, you pay only for the nodes you use.

5. Which of the following is a benefit of In-Memory caching?
   Answer: D

   Helps you launch clusters quickly to store regularly used data.

6. What is Elastic Load Balancing?
   Answer: C

   Elastic Load Balancing is a highly available AWS compute service that enables greater fault tolerance levels by distributing traffic across a group of EC2 instances in one or multiple AZs.

7. What is a Relational Database?
   Answer: C

   Relational Database is the most commonly used database type that offers a common interface where users can read/write from the database through queries/commands written using SQL.

8. What is the structure of an ElastiCache Redis Replication Group?
   Answer: D

   An ElastiCache cluster for the master node with extra clusters as replicas, and each of those clusters with a single node.

9. What are Prime Candidates for Caching?
Answer: B

Often, data elements accessed on every page load or with every request, but remain unchanged are the prime candidates for caching.

10. What is a Maintenance Window?
Answer: C

Maintenance Window is the 60 minute time duration specified by the customer when either requested or required software patching occurs in Amazon ElastiCache.

11. What is the characteristic of an SQS Delay Queue?
Answer: B

SQS Delay Queue is a feature that lets you postpone delivery of messages in a queue for a defined period of time, making messages invisible to consumers for that delay period.

12. Which of the following is a scaling mechanism for Memcached ElastiCache cluster?
Answer: D

Add nodes to the cluster.

13. How many read replicas can be created per ElastiCache Master Cluster?
Answer: B

You can create upto 5 read replicas for any primary cache node in ElastiCache.

14. What is a use case for Redis?
Answer: A

Redis can be used for Data backup and restore options.

15. Which of the following is a benefit of caching for databases?
Answer: C

Offloading read requests to the cache tier will alleviate pressure.

16. Which of the following describes how Memcached Auto Discovery works?
Answer: C

ElastiCache cluster gets a unique configuration endpoint.

17. Which of the following statements is true?
Answer: C

If a software patching is included in the maintenance, ElastiCache Nodes might face downtime during the maintenance window.

18. Which of the following statements is true?
Answer: D

Both ElastiCache cluster types, Memcached and Redis, can be expanded vertically by choosing a smaller or larger node type that matches your needs.

19. How can Prime Candidates for Caching be identified?
Answer: C

Prime candidate elements can be identified by analyzing patterns of data usage, regularly run queries, and expensive operations.

20. Tom wants to access an ElastiCache node from the public internet, how should Tom access an ElastiCache node?
Answer: A

You cannot access an ElastiCache node from the public internet, you must be within the EC2 network, and authorized through relevant security groups.

21. Meg wants to change an Elasti-Cache cluster's instance type, what should Meg know about changing node instance types of ElastiCache clusters?

Answer: D

You cannot dynamically change an ElastiCache cluster's node instance type, but you can create a new cluster when you scale up or down.

# 25

# Answers To Additional Services

1. What is the maximum size of a Kinesis record's data blob?
Answer: D

The maximum size of a Kinesis record's data blob is 1 MB.

2. Which of the following describes what Amazon CloudFront is suitable for?
Answer: B

Amazon CloudFront is suitable for: Popular dynamic and static content where users are distributed geographically.

3. Which of the following can be considered as information recorded by CloudTrail?
Answer: C

Name of the API

4. What is the ideal mix for Clusters used in app testing?
Answer: D

Clusters used in app testing: Master: spot; Core: spot; Task: spot

5. Which of the following is a CloudFront Origin Setting?
Answer: D

Origin Domain Name

6. Which of the following is an AWS Storage and Content Delivery Service?
Answer: D

Amazon CloudFront

7. Which of the following is a Geo Restriction option in CloudFront?
Answer: A

Using CloudFront Geo Restriction feature: restricts access to all files associated with a distribution, at a country level.

8. What is the maximum amount of data that can be stored in Gateway-Cached appliances?
Answer: C

Gateway-Cached volume: 1 PB (32 volumes, each 32 TB in size)

9. Christian wants to reserve CloudFront capacity, what are the reserved capacity pricing options that Christian should be aware of?
Answer: C

CloudFront offers reserved capacity pricing in which you get a considerable discount by committing to a minimum monthly usage level for 12 months or more.

10. Which of the following is a functionality that can be configured in a CloudFront Cache Behavior?
Answer: D

Functionalities that can be configured in a CloudFront Cache Behavior: Origin for forwarding requests (for multi-origin distributions).

11. Which of the following is an OpsWorks Lifecycle event?
Answer: C

Setup

12. What is the maximum capacity of a Storage Gateway VTL?
Answer: B

You can store upto 1500 virtual tapes in a Storage Gateway VTL, not exceeding the maximum size limit of 150 TB.

13. What is the maximum size of Gateway-Stored volume?
Answer: B

16 TB

14. Which of the following describes a Use Case of CloudFront Signed Cookie?
Answer: A

CloudFront Signed Cookies - Use Cases: If you do not want your current URLs changed.

15. What is AWS Storage Gateway?
Answer: D

AWS Storage Gateway is a service that connects your IT environment with AWS storage infrastructure, maintains regularly accessed data on-premises, and encrypts and stores all data on S3 or Glacier.

16. Which of the following is an origin supported by Amazon CloudFront?
Answer: D

Amazon S3 websites

17. Which of the following statements is true?
Answer: C

Storage Gateway Virtual Tape Libraries are stored on Amazon S3, and Storage Gateway Virtual Tape Shelves are stored on Amazon Glacier.

18. Which of the following is a component of AWS Elastic Beanstalk?
Answer: B

Environment

19. Which of the following is a configuration of AWS Storage Gateway?
Answer: C

Gateway-Cached

20. What is AWS CloudTrail?
Answer: D

AWS CloudTrail is a security service that makes user activity visible by recording API calls made on your account, helping you track changes made to your resources.

21. Chris wants to use CloudFront to serve dynamic content, what should Chris know of dynamic content on CloudFront?
Answer: B

You can now use CloudFront to serve dynamic content, making applications faster and more responsive, irrespective of where your users are situated.

22. Which of the following is an Import source supported by AWS Import/Export?
Answer: D

Amazon S3

23. Which of the following is a scaling option for OpsWorks instances?
Answer: C

Time-based

24. Which of the following statements is true?

Answer: B

You can integrate CloudHSM with Amazon RDS only for Oracle instances, allowing AWS to operate Oracle databases while you still control master encryption keys.

25. Which of the following is a type of AWS Import/Export?

Answer: D

AWS Snowball

26. Which of the following is a Use Case for Amazon Kinesis Firehose?

Answer: D

Firehose: Loading huge volumes of streaming data into AWS.

27. Chris wants to use a Storage Gateway snapshot to create an EBS volume, what should Chris know about using Storage Gateway snapshot to create EBS volume?

Answer: A

Amazon allows you to take point-in-time snapshots of Gateway-Cached volume data in Amazon S3 in the form of Amazon EBS snapshots.

28. Which of the following is a type of Amazon Kinesis Service?

Answer: C

Amazon Kinesis Firehose

29. Which of the following is a language supported by Elastic Beanstalk?

Answer: B

Node.js

30. Which of the following is an option for CloudFront to deliver HTTPS content in the client's domain name?

Answer: D

Dedicated IP custom SSL

31. Which of the following describes a method with which CloudFront can serve private content?

Answer: B

Signed URLs

32. Which of the following is a step describing how Amazon CloudFront works?

Answer: B

Amazon CloudFront first uses geolocation to identify geographic locations of users and optimize downloads.

33. Which of the following is a benefit of CloudFront?

Answer: A

Low latency

34. Which of the following describes when to use AWS Directory Service for Microsoft Active Directory?

Answer: C

When there are more than 5000 users.

35. Which of the following can be described as a part of the CloudFront Distribution Details?

Answer: A

Default Root Object

36. What is the Use Case of a Gateway-Cached volume?

Answer: A

Gateway-Cached: Expands on-premises storage to S3, and caches frequently used files locally.

37. What is the ideal mix for Long-running EMR Clusters?

Answer: B

Long-running EMR clusters: Master: on-demand; Core: on-demand; Task: spot

38. Which of the following statements is true?
Answer: A

Tapes ejected by backup software from a VTL are moved to a VTS located in Glacier, for long-term storage/archiving purposes.

39. What is Key Management?
Answer: D

Key Management is the management of cryptographic keys in a cryptosystem which includes their creation, exchange, use, storage, and replacement.

40. Which of the following is an AWS OpsWorks Component that can be defined by the customer?
Answer: C

Architecture of an application

41. Mike wants to upload content through CloudFront, how should Mike attempt this?
Answer: D

You can now upload content to your web servers through Cloud-Front using the existing distributions for upload requests by turning on support in the AWS MC.

42. What is Geo restriction in Cloud-Front?
Answer: C

Geo restriction in CloudFront is a feature through which you can block users in specific locations from accessing content being distributed through your CloudFront web distribution.

43. Which of the following is an available Elastic Beanstalk environment tier?
Answer: D

Web Server Tier

44. What is an AWS Directory Service?
Answer: B

AWS Directory Service is a managed service that provides directories containing information about a client organization like the users, computers, groups, and other resources.

# 26

# Answers To Security

1. What is the type of Cryptography that is used in Amazon EC2?
Answer: D

EC2 uses public-key cryptography, which means a public key is used to encrypt data, and a private key is used by the recipient to decrypt data.

2. Which of the following is a characteristic of a Security Group Rule?
Answer: C

Deny by default

3. How can High-Availability Design within AWS be achieved?
Answer: D

High-Availability Design within AWS can be achieved by distributing applications across various Availability Zones which helps build resilience towards a lot of system failure modes.

4. Which of the following statements is true?
Answer: D

Securing Connections: Connections between your DB Instance and your application can be encrypted using SSL.

5. What is AWS CloudTrail?
Answer: B

AWS CloudTrail is a security service that makes user activity visible by recording API calls made on your account, helping you track changes made to your resources.

6. Which of the following best describes what rotation of keys can secure?
Answer: A

IAM User Accounts

7. Which of the following describes a step to access the WorkSpaces?
Answer: B

WorkSpaces grants access to users only after they successfully sign in with either their Active Directory credentials, or a set of unique credentials.

8. Which of the following statements is true?
Answer: D

Access Control: Access to Instances can be controlled via DB security groups.

9. Which of the following statements is true?

Answer: C

AWS does not allow EC2 instances running in promiscuous mode to sniff traffic that is targeted for some other virtual instance.

10. What is Loose Coupling?
Answer: B

Loose Coupling is the practice of coupling system components as loosely as possible to reduce inter-dependencies, which in turn prevents failure of other components when one fails.

11. Which of the following statements is true?
Answer: D

Security Standards and Certifications AWS is in compliance with: * FISMA * DIACAP * ISO 9001, ISO 27001, and ISO 27018

12. Which of the following statements is true?
Answer: A

You can associate one or more security groups to one or more of your EC2 instances at the time of launching the instances, and also add/modify rules later.

13. Which of the following statements is true?
Answer: B

Network traffic in EC2 instances cannot be spoofed as AWS permits instances to send traffic using only their own MAC/source IP addresses.

14. Which of the following statements is true?
Answer: C

To grant initial access to an instance, EC2 supports RSA 2048 SSH-2 Key pairs.

15. Which of the following is an AWS service that supports encryption of data at rest?
Answer: D

Amazon S3

16. Mark wants to connect to EC2 Instances on Linux using key pairs, how should Mark attempt this?
Answer: A

As Linux instances don't have passwords, you login using the SSH private key.

17. Which of the following is a Security and Identity service offered by AWS?
Answer: A

AWS IAM

18. Which of the following is an authentic protocol supported by Amazon WorkSpaces?
Answer: C

RADIUS

19. Which of the following statements is true?
Answer: D

Access to SQS is granted or denied only based on the AWS account, or a user created via AWS IAM.

20. Which of the following is a security feature within Amazon VPC?
Answer: A

Security groups

21. Which of the following is a key in Amazon Redshift Encryption Architecture?
Answer: D

Data encryption keys

22. How can controlling network access to ElastiCache Cache Clusters be achieved?
Answer: C

You can control network access to your ElastiCache Cache Clusters through Cache Security Groups which play the role of a firewall.

23. Which of the following is a type of credential used by AWS for authentication?
Answer: A

MFA

24. Which of the following can be described as a security feature on Amazon S3?
Answer: A

Access on S3 is restricted by default, letting only owners of S3 buckets the rights.

25. Which of the following is a step for Amazon Cognito to provide identity and sync services for mobile and web-based applications?
Answer: D

Amazon Cognito returns a new ID, and new temporary AWS credentials with restricted privileges, to the user.

26. What are API endpoints in AWS?
Answer: A

API endpoints in AWS are customer access points placed by AWS that allow secure sessions via HTTPS access, enabling you to monitor inbound/outbound network traffic more comprehensively.

27. What is a Key Pair?
Answer: C

Private and public keys together are called a key pair, which you create while logging in to your instance the first time, and specify at the time of each launch.

28. Which of the following is a step for Amazon Cognito to provide identity and sync services for mobile and web-based applications?
Answer: D

Client application authenticates with an identity provider (e.g. Google) using their SDK.

29. What is the Shared Responsibility Model?
Answer: B

Shared Responsibility model is a security model used by AWS where AWS ensures security of the cloud infrastructure, and requires customers to secure workloads deployed in their AWS accounts.

30. Billy is exploring effects of attempting unauthorized port scans on EC2, what should Billy know about unauthorized port scans on EC2?
Answer: C

The AWS Acceptable Use Policy which every customer is bound by holds them in violation of the policy if they are found performing unauthorized port scans.

31. Amy wants to configure an EC2 security group to deny traffic, what should Amy know about configuring EC2 security groups?
Answer: C

An EC2 security group can only be configured to allow specific rules, not to deny any, and separate rules can be configured for outbound and inbound traffic.

32. Which of the following statements is true?
Answer: B

Securing Data-In-Transit: Asynchronous transfer of data over SSL. Securing Data-At-Rest: Encryption using AES-256 (For data stored in S3).

33. How should Access Keys be stored?

Answer: D

Dos for storing Access Keys: If you have a large fleet of EC2 instances, use IAM roles as a secure way of distributing keys.

34. How are EBS volumes and snapshots encrypted?

Answer: B

EBS volumes and snapshots are encrypted using AES-256 which encrypts data on servers hosting EC2 instances, ensuring security while data moves between EC2 and EBS.

*27*

# Answers To Risk Management and Compliance

1. Which of the following statements is true?

   Answer: C

   Ways in which AWS educates customers about AWS security and control environment: By supplying certificates, reports, etc. directly to customers.

2. Which of the following statements is true?

   Answer: A

   Steps to Achieve Strong Compliance and Governance in AWS: * Identify and keep record of all 3rd party owned controls. * Ensure all control objectives are met.

3. Which of the following is an AWS Global Geographic region?

   Answer: C

   South America (Sao Paulo).

4. What is the Shared Responsibility model?

   Answer: C

   Shared Responsibility model is a security model used by AWS where AWS ensures security of the cloud infrastructure, and requires customers to secure workloads deployed in their AWS accounts.

5. Which of the following is a prominent compliance certification of AWS?

   Answer: C

   FIPS 140-2.

6. Which of the following is a way in which AWS provides IT Control Information to customers?

   Answer: A

   Specific control definition.

7. What is the number of geographic regions that AWS Cloud operates from?

   Answer: B

   16

8. Which of the following is a step to achieve strong compliance and governance in AWS?

   Answer: D

   Step 1: Review all available information about the IT environment, and document all compliance requirements.

9. What is the Shared Responsibility in AWS IT controls?

   Answer: C

   Shared responsibility in AWS is extended to IT controls where the management, operation, and verification of IT controls is done with AWS handling controls for physical infrastructure, and customer managing those for guest OS's.

10. Which of the following describes a way in which AWS educates customers about AWS security and control environment?
Answer: B

By acquiring industry standard certifications and 3rd party attestations.

11. Which of the following is a step to achieve strong compliance and governance in AWS?
Answer: D

Devise and enforce control objectives that are in line with compliance requirements.

12. What is an AWS Business Risk Plan?
Answer: C

AWS Business Risk Plan is a plan developed by the AWS risk management team that identifies risks and enforces controls to manage/mitigate them.

13. Which of the following can be considered as a core area of the AWS Risk and Compliance Program?
Answer: D

Risk management

14. What are the characteristics of IT Governance in AWS?
Answer: B

IT Governance in AWS is where the customer is responsible for maintaining proper governance across the IT control environment, irrespective of the deployment type (cloud/on-premises/hybrid).

15. Which of the following is a component of AWS Control Environment?
Answer: C

Technology.

# Answers To Architectural Best Practices

1. Which of the following statements is true?
   Answer: D

   Stateless Applications are applications which require no information on past interactions, and do not store session data.

2. Which of the following statements is true?
   Answer: C

   List of AWS Architecture Best Practices: * Designing for failure. * Decoupling application components.

3. How can building a highly available architecture on AWS be achieved?
   Answer: A

   A Highly available architecture on AWS can be achieved by building systems that can withstand the failure of single or multiple components.

4. What are the characteristics of Active Redundancy?
   Answer: D

   Active Redundancy distributes requests to multiple redundant resources so that if a resource fails, others can take on the extra workload, and causes no downtime.

5. Which of the following is a benefit of Bootstrapping?
   Answer: B

   You can quickly recreate environments with less effort.

6. What are the characteristics of Vertical Scaling?
   Answer: A

   Vertical Scaling cannot work beyond certain limits, and hence is not a highly available or cost-effective way.

7. What is Loose Coupling?
   Answer: B

   Loose Coupling is the practice of coupling system components as loosely as possible to reduce inter-dependencies, which in turn prevents failure of other components when one fails.

8. Which of the following is an IT architecture scaling option?
   Answer: D

   Vertical Scaling.

9. Which of the following is a benefit of Bootstrapping?
   Answer: A

Retain more control over your resources.

10. What are the characteristics of Elastic Architecture?
Answer: B

Elastic Architecture is an IT architecture that supports increase in traffic, data size, or users, without a dip in performance.

11. What does leveraging different storage options imply?
Answer: C

Leverage Different Storage Options is the practice of choosing different options (from several storage options offered by AWS) to suit different types of datasets, to optimize performance and save costs.

12. Which of the following statements is true?
Answer: A

Standby Redundancy uses the failover process to recover functionality on a secondary resource when a resource fails, and causes downtime during the failover process.

13. How can Horizontal Scaling be achieved?
Answer: D

Horizontal Scaling can be achieved by increasing the number of resources.

www.ingramcontent.com/pod-product-compliance
Lightning Source LLC
Chambersburg PA
CBHW051240050326
40689CB00007B/1010